This journal belongs to

_____

Year

_____

SACRED MARKINGS

MATTHEW R. LYNSKEY

NOBLE IMPRINT
a publishing collaborative

Sacred Markings: Journaling Toward Second Nature
© 2021 by Matthew R. Lynskey. All rights reserved.

Published by Noble Imprint (www.nobleimprint.com) under license agreement.

All rights reserved. No part of this work may be reproduced or transmitted in any form or by any means, electronic or mechanical, including photocopying and recording, or by any means of any information storage or retrieval system, without the expressed written permission of the publisher.

Scripture quotations are from the ESV® Bible (The Holy Bible, English Standard Version®), copyright 2001 by Crossway, a publishing ministry of Good News Publishers. Used by permission. All rights reserved.

Library of Congress Cataloging-in-Publication Data is available upon request.

ISBN: 978-1-956144-00-0
Standard hardcover edition

Printed in the United States of America

25 24 23 22 21   10 9 8 7 6 5 4 3 2 1

"Habits soon become a second nature; to form new ones is hard work; but those formed in youth remain in old age." [1]

Charles H. Spurgeon, "Obadiah"

"What is customary becomes pleasant, in so far as it becomes natural: because custom is like a second nature." [2]

Thomas Aquinas, *Summa Theologica*

"Custom is a second nature which destroys the former. But what is nature? For is custom not natural? I am much afraid that nature is itself only a first custom, as custom is a second nature." [3]

Blaise Pascal, *Pensées*

Table of Contents

9
Preface

10
Introduction
Surveying the Landscape
of *Sacred Markings*

20
Grand Examen
Navigating the Terrain
of the Spiritual Life

22	*Session 1:*	**IDENTITY**
36	*Session 2:*	**VOCATION**
50	*Session 3:*	**MISSION**
64	*Session 4:*	**COMMUNITY**
78	*Session 5:*	**VALUES**
92	*Session 6:*	**HABITS**

106
Seasonal Review
Keeping Log of
Personal Progress

110	*Quarter 1*
124	*Quarter 2*
138	*Quarter 3*
152	*Quarter 4*

166
Personal Memoirs
Sensing God's Movement
in the Daily Journey

274
Further Resources
Charting the Course
for Ongoing Formation

"So teach us to number our days that we may get a heart of wisdom."

Psalm 90:12

Preface

The stewardship of your life is one of your highest callings. First and foremost, God is calling you to himself: to enjoy a *reconciled relationship* with your Creator. Amazingly, he is inviting you into a *meaningful community*: to relish deep fellowship with other believers. Further, God is commissioning you into *worldwide mission*: to live out your vocation in the world as an ambassador of Christ for global impact. Without paying meaningful attention to your life—your identity, vocation, mission, community, values, and habits—it is possible for you to squander God's best for you. The meaningful stewardship of our lives is a mark of spiritual maturity.

To guard us from living unpremeditated lives—the tragedy of an *un-stewarded life*—God has gifted us with the capacity for self-reflection. Regardless of your stage in life, you have a divine duty to steward your life with prudence and foresight. Personal reflection itself, however, does not guarantee a meaningful or a wise life. We enjoy a substantive life as we allow God's Word to serve as a mirror for our lives. Imprinted in the very constitution of the Scriptures is a vision of life after God's intended design. Wisdom is gained as we allow the anatomy of the biblical text to expose the disjointedness of our lives and realign us into God's order.

Many obstacles threaten meaningful personal reflection: cluttered schedules leaving no margin for contemplation, apathetic spirits having lost the gravity of eternity, painful trauma we have internally suppressed, self-reliance crusted with inflated self-confidence, fiery zeal absent of accountability, or good intentions without a clear vision to realize them. We must buffet against these attacks, seeing personal self-examination interwoven with life stewardship in community as one of our most significant investments.

As a contribution to help in this process, *Sacred Markings* offers guided exercises blended with open journal space to assist you as you grapple with eternally weighty ideas that relate to your own personal story. The following pages are offered as a pathway toward spiritual maturity. The moment is now to bring the "time of your life" under the scrutiny of God's Word.

Matthew R. Lynskey
Noble City Church
July 2021

Introduction

Surveying the Landscape of *Sacred Markings*

Sacred Markings is a journal designed to chronicle your journey in the Christian faith. It is meant to help you be a thoughtful and faithful steward of your life. Exploring the following **Introduction**, take a moment to orient yourself to the purpose, layout, and use of this journal. Allow the following pages to sketch a spiritual formation process that seeks to cultivate various dimensions of your life in an integrated and holistic process of personal reflection.

Introduction

Following Christ should be second nature! In Ephesians 4:22-24, Paul gives the summons "to put off your old self, which belongs to your former manner of life and is corrupt through deceitful desires, and to be renewed in the spirit of your minds, and to put on the new self, created after the likeness of God in true righteousness and holiness." Walking as a Christ follower involves "putting off" our *old selves* and "putting on" our *new selves* in Christ. In the gospel, God remakes our first nature, born in the corruption of sin, into the likeness of Christ. In Christ, our first nature is being restored and we are "becoming second nature" in the image of Christ. This work of "becoming second nature" in Christ is a divine work of God's *sacred marking* in our lives.

But *sacred marking* in what sense? First, *our lives are marked by God.* Being fashioned in the image of God, God has "custom made" each of us to be his noble image-bearers in his world. Through sustained reflection and dialogue, this journal helps disciples of Christ discern their nobility and uniqueness as God's image-bearers. Second, *we should mark out our spiritual journey as a means to trace God's work in our lives.* One of the ways we can learn of God's sacred marking in our lives is by recording insights—written reflections, scriptural musings, thoughtful notations—about our spiritual journey. Like field notes to the Christian life, this journal provides space to make "markings" of what we are learning about ourselves, God, and our role in God's plan. Lastly, we are to embrace God's call on our lives *to leave a mark in his world.* As much as this journal is designed to help us realize God's work in us, it is also made to help us take intentional steps to live out our unique mission to leave a mark in God's world. What, then, are *sacred markings*? Sacred markings involve God's mark *on us*, God's mark *in us*, and God's mark *through us!* In short, *God intends to work through you as he works in you.*

God's dynamic work *in us* and *through us* takes place in various spheres of life. Like concentric circles that reverberate outward, God activates individual growth, family order, church maturity, and world engagement (see Figure 1). We must train our spiritual sensitivities to discern how God is extending his sovereign hand in each of these life arenas.

Throughout history, many notable historical figures from various walks of life kept notebooks, sketch pads, diaries, or journals to mark their lives: artist and inventor Leonardo da Vinci, general and president George Washington, explorers Lewis and Clark, renowned author Lewis

Life Spheres
Figure 1

INDIVIDUAL — Growth in personal character, conduct, beliefs, discipline, habits, and attitudes.

FAMILY — Health within marriage, parenting, sibling, and extended family relationships.

CHURCH — Maturity of gifts, service, roles, and responsibilities in local church community.

WORLD — Meaningful engagement of neighborhood, societal, global, and spiritual realities.

Carroll, well-known composer Pyotr Ilyich Tchaikovsky, ground-breaking scientist Marie Curie, slave and (then) free man Michael Shiner, young girl-in-hiding Anne Frank, diplomat and economist Dag Hammarskjöld, and many more. Throughout the history of the church, many Christians have practiced journaling as a means to chronicle, or *mark*, their own spiritual journeys. Figures such as theologian Jonathan Edwards, missionary Jim Elliot, hymnist Charles Wesley, Puritan preacher and theologian Isaac Ambrose, preacher George Whitefield, Bible translator William Carey, and activist and martyr Dietrich Bonhoeffer. Such journal writing enabled Christians to explore theological reflection, record mission endeavors, trace progress in life and ministry, and cultivate personal piety. In the vein of such a great historical precedent, *Sacred Markings* is a journal that seeks to aid Christians in the progress of their spiritual life.

As a believer, you are an extension of an intergenerational Christian faith. The Christian faith was always meant to be experienced in community. Your growth is connected to the investment previous generations will make in your own development. Envision your life as an important link in passing down the faith to the next generation! This journal seeks to bring intentional conversation between generations of disciples in settings such as mentoring relationships, community gatherings, family conversations, and/or leadership assessment and training. *Sacred Markings* is a tool that enables disciples of Jesus to journal their journey of "becoming second nature" in Christ together in community.

How to Use This Journal

This journal offers a blend of biblical reflection, guided exercises, templated practices, and creative space which all serve your spiritual formation in the context of meaningful Christian relationships. In short, it is a tool for *life stewardship in community*. Attempting to curate a journal that would represent a unique mixture of directed activities for personal development and flexible open space for personal reflection, we aspired to facilitate an experience that would help you recognize God's mark *on you*, discern God's mark *in you*, and envision the mark God wants to make *through you*.

Sacred Markings is both designed for you to record some of your most important insights about your life after sustained, concentrated reflection as well as to mark some of your more incidental thoughts about life along the way. (Importantly, sometimes our mere incidental thoughts prove to be more important than we at first realize.) This journal helps you chronicle your spiritual journey. Each journal covers one year, aiding you to document your own personal faith pilgrimage.

With that in mind, we sought to give opportunities for you to record your own thoughts as well as for trusted mentors and members of the Christian community to record their assessment of your spiritual journey. Like field notes sketched by an on-site researcher, this journal represents space to gain clarity on your past, make meaningful observations about your present, and take courageous, faith-filled steps toward the future. By completing the journal on an annual cycle, it not only seeks to provide a periodic means to chronicle your faith journey, but also a means to build a framework for how to think about life according to sacred rhythms (see Figure 2). In sum, we have sought to budget the space in this journal in purposeful ways to round out a process of personal formation. In what follows, we offer a brief overview of the structure of the journal and some suggested practices for its use.

The Grand Examen: Taking an Annual View of Our Lives

In the first portion of this journal, we invite disciples to a **Grand Examen** of their lives. By investigating six major facets to human nature—identity, vocation, mission, community, priorities, and habits—each person undergoes an annual, personal "life appraisal." Allowing the book of Ephesians to help us take inventory of our lives, disciples explore (together with other disciples) some major questions of life: Who am I? (Ephesians 1); What am I called to do? (Ephesians 2); Why am I here? (Ephesians 3); Where do I belong? (Ephesians 4); Which things are of greatest importance? (Ephesians 5); and How will I move forward? (Ephesians 6).

Sacred Rhythms
Figure 2

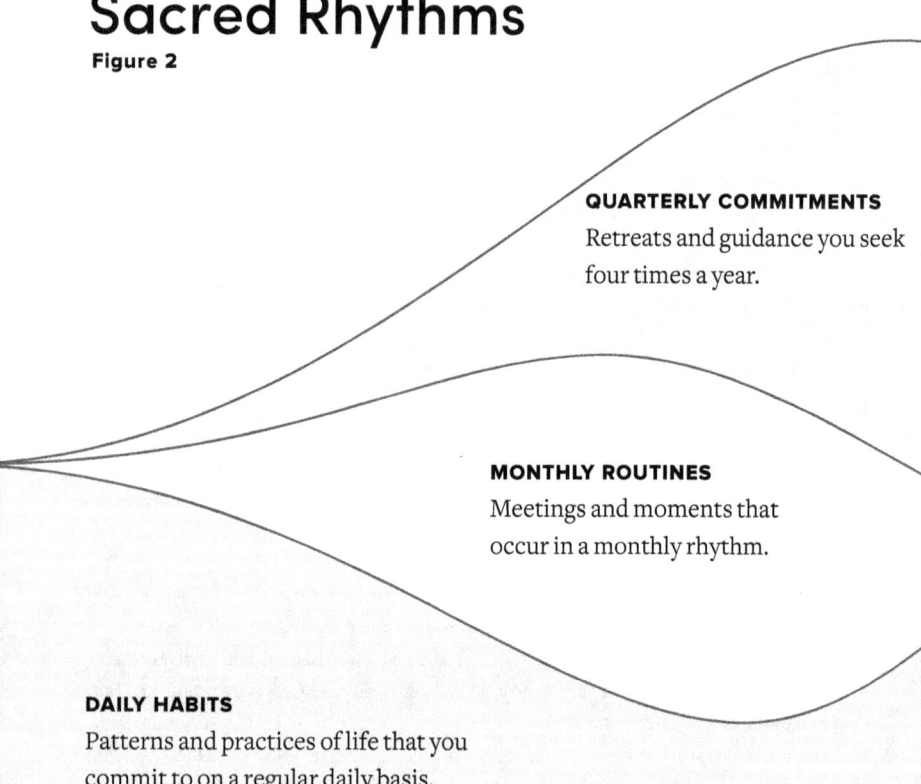

QUARTERLY COMMITMENTS
Retreats and guidance you seek four times a year.

MONTHLY ROUTINES
Meetings and moments that occur in a monthly rhythm.

DAILY HABITS
Patterns and practices of life that you commit to on a regular daily basis.

Like tributaries that careen into a cross-continental riverbed, these six dimensions of human experience form a mainstay for how we experience life. In this annual self-examination, each of the six sessions has a consistent fivefold structure: Hearing the Word (pondering what God says in Ephesians); Seeking for Wisdom (considering counsel from the wider Christian community); Grasping the Idea (interacting with the theme at a concept level); Discovering Your Design (recording your approach to life); and Chronicling the Journey (narrating your personal progress). Representing the first movement of the journal, these six sessions as a whole could be completed at your own personal pace, as a weekly series, during the concentrated blitz of a retreat, or within the regular rhythm of a mentoring relationship. On the main, these sessions work best, done once a year, when there is sufficient time for honest and sustained reflection, combined with church community input and dialogue, as disciples consider how God wants to recalibrate their individual and community life.

LIFETIME EXPERIENCES
Events and experiences you hope to have once in a lifetime.

ANNUAL VENTURES
Projects or training that you attend to on a yearly basis.

Seasonal Review: Returning to Life's Big Questions on a Quarterly Basis
After taking a "deep dive" into the big questions of life, disciples are ready to begin thinking about quarterly rhythms to their upcoming year. In the second movement of this journal, we offer life assessments, planning templates, and open space where mentors and church community members can record your progress across the seasons of the year. These quarterly reflections are a sequel to your annual **Grand Examen**. Moreover, they are meant to be done in the context of community and mentoring relationships. Having a log of your own "markings" will prove to be valuable as you grow in your faith. However, being able to capture the comments, insights, exhortations, encouragements, and advice from key mentors in your life in a common place will prove to be priceless. One of the best ways to track your progress over the course of the year is to try to connect (over a meal!) with a mentor or mentoring couple on a regular basis. These conversations could culminate in an honest dialogue over your quarterly assessment, reflecting on your progress in the previous months and discussing intentional plans for growth in the upcoming months.

Personal Memoirs: Tracking Our Lives within Weekly and Daily Movements
The spiritual practice of journaling affords a unique opportunity to chronicle our faith journey. While it is important to consider broad categories that affect the overall trajectory of one's life, it is also important to detail happenings that occur in life's smaller moments. Toward this end, *Sacred Markings* encourages you to journal about your faith development on a weekly and daily basis.

Weekly Summaries. A helpful way to pursue quarterly progress is to cultivate weekly habits. Using the six categories from the annual **Grand Examen**—identity, vocation, mission, community, priorities, and habits—blank journal space (customizable for many uses) is provided for disciples to briefly reflect on each category in light of the past week. This is not only a helpful milestone toward quarterly "check-ins" but also builds a framework that will help you think about your life. These weekly ruminations could be a great spiritual exercise for practicing Sabbath, a conversational blueprint for family worship, a community guide for your church's weekly gatherings, or a shepherding tool for mentoring relationships. The weekly template guide in the back of the journal (page 280) offers a scope of what these specific questions would entail.

Daily Reflections. Daily reflection is facilitated in this journal with the same blank journal space, also allocated for daily spiritual practices (i.e., reading, prayer, journaling, etc.) or other annotations that would be helpful throughout your day. Remember, this is a tool to help chronicle your journey. So, consider using this section of blank pages as open processing space for any variety of questions, reflections, observations, or insights that you discover along the way. The daily template guides in the back of the journal (page 276 and 278) facilitate morning and evening communion with God.

Further Resources: Committing to Lifelong Learning
At the end of this journal there are a collection of recommended resources that can aid you in your ongoing spiritual development. We have provided Bible reading exercises, templates of spiritual practices, and an essentials reading library to furnish and outfit you with resources for a

lifelong process of growth and development. While the *Sacred Markings* journal is meant to build a "framework of life" by its year-to-year consistency, these additional tools will help you begin to build a library of key resources that will stimulate your spiritual life with variety and depth.

In the end, this journal is just a tool. As the concept for this journal was birthed, we envisioned a tool to help disciples reflectively engage the Scriptures, prayerfully seek God's presence, meaningfully guide mentoring relationships, deeply enjoy community camaraderie, substantively assess leadership training, and proactively make the best use of their time. If any of these aspirations are able to be realized, in part or in full, then may all thanks be to God who has marked us that we would leave "sacred markings" in his world as we *carpe diem* ("seize the day"), mindful to do so *coram deo* ("in the presence of God")!

Grand Examen

Navigating the Terrain of the Spiritual Life

....

The first movement of this journal guides you through a **Grand Examen** of your life. Designed as a yearly reflection on your faith journey, the following six sessions take a tour through each of the chapters in the book of Ephesians, exploring six vital undercurrents of our spiritual life: identity, vocation, mission, community, priorities, and habits. Each session has five mini-movements:

- *Hearing the Word*: pondering what God says in Ephesians
- *Seeking for Wisdom*: considering counsel from the wider Christian community
- *Grasping the Idea*: interacting with the theme at a concept level
- *Discovering Our Design*: recording your approach to life
- *Chronicling the Journey*: narrating your personal progress

Identity
Who am I?

"You are the salt of the earth, but if salt has lost its taste, how shall its saltiness be restored?"

Matthew 5:13

"Man knows that his I is real only in the relation with the Thou."[4]

Dietrich Bonhoeffer, *The Communion of the Saints*

○┐ **Hearing the Word**

Rooting Your Identity in Christ

¹:¹ Paul, an apostle of Christ Jesus by the will of God, To the saints who are in Ephesus, and are faithful in Christ Jesus: ² Grace to you and peace from God our Father and the Lord Jesus Christ.

³ Blessed be the God and Father of our Lord Jesus Christ, who has blessed us in Christ with every spiritual blessing in the heavenly places, ⁴ even as he chose us in him before the foundation of the world, that we should be holy and blameless before him. In love ⁵ he predestined us for adoption to himself as sons through Jesus Christ, according to the purpose of his will, ⁶ to the praise of his glorious grace, with which he has blessed us in the Beloved. ⁷ In him we have redemption through his blood, the forgiveness of our trespasses, according to the riches of his grace, ⁸ which he lavished upon us, in all wisdom and insight ⁹ making known to us the mystery of his will, according to his purpose, which he set forth in Christ ¹⁰ as a plan for the fullness of time, to unite all things in him, things in heaven and things on earth.

¹¹ In him we have obtained an inheritance, having been predestined according to the purpose of him who works all things according to the counsel of his will, ¹² so that we who were the first to hope in Christ might be to the praise of his glory. ¹³ In him you also, when you heard the word of truth, the gospel of your salvation, and believed in him, were sealed with the promised Holy Spirit, ¹⁴ who is the guarantee of our inheritance until we acquire possession of it, to the praise of his glory.

¹⁵ For this reason, because I have heard of your faith in the Lord Jesus and your love toward all the saints, ¹⁶ I do not cease to give thanks for you, remembering you in my prayers, ¹⁷ that the God of our Lord Jesus Christ, the Father of glory, may give you the Spirit of wisdom and of revelation in the knowledge of him, ¹⁸ having the eyes of your hearts enlightened, that you may know what is the hope to which he has called you, what are the riches of his glorious inheritance in the saints, ¹⁹ and what is the immeasurable greatness of his power toward us who believe, according to the working of his great might ²⁰ that he worked in Christ when he raised him from the dead and seated him at his right hand in the heavenly places, ²¹ far above all rule and authority and power and dominion, and above every name that is named, not only in this age but also in the one to come. ²² And he put all things under his feet and gave him as head over all things to the church, ²³ which is his body, the fullness of him who fills all in all.

Ephesians 1:1–23

Reflect

As a believer, what is your true identity in Christ? Take some time to prayerfully read Ephesians 1:1–23 and then record your insights.

Seeking for Wisdom

Discovering Your Real Self in Christ

"The more we get what we now call 'ourselves' out of the way and let Him [Christ] take us over, the more truly ourselves we become....In that sense our real selves are all waiting for us in Him. It is no good trying to 'be myself' without Him. The more I resist Him and try to live on my own, the more I become dominated by my own heredity and upbringing and surroundings and natural desires...It is when I turn to Christ, when I give myself up to His Personality, that I first begin to have a real personality of my own....Until you have given up your self to Him you will not have a real self....Your real, new self (which is Christ's and also yours, and yours just because it is His) will not come as long as you are looking for it. It will come when you are looking for Him...The principle runs through all life from top to bottom. Give up yourself, and you will find your real self. Lose your life and you will save it. Submit to death, death of your ambitions and favourite wishes every day and death of your whole body in the end: submit with every fibre of your being, and you will find eternal life. Keep back nothing. Nothing that you have not given away will be really yours. Nothing in you that has not died will ever be raised from the dead. Look for yourself, and you will find in the long run only hatred, loneliness, despair, rage, ruin, and decay. But look for Christ and you will find Him, and with Him everything else thrown in."[5]

C. S. Lewis, *Mere Christianity*

Explore

How do these quotes shape your understanding of your Christian identity? After thoughtfully reading these quotes and exploring key ideas in community discussion, record your insights below.

Compelled to Look Upward

"Our wisdom, in so far as it ought to be deemed true and solid wisdom, consists almost entirely of two parts: the knowledge of God and of ourselves...For, in the first place, no man can survey himself without [at once] turning his thoughts towards the God in whom he lives and moves; because it is perfectly obvious, that the endowments which we possess cannot possibly be from ourselves... [Our] very being is nothing else than subsistence in God alone...In particular, the miserable ruin into which the revolt of the first man has plunged us, compels us to turn our eyes upwards...[Every] man, being stung by the consciousness of his own unhappiness, in this way necessarily obtains at least some knowledge of God...We are accordingly urged by our own evil things to consider the good things of God; and, indeed, we cannot aspire to Him in earnest until we have begun to be displeased with ourselves...Every person, therefore, on coming to the knowledge of himself, is not only urged to seek God, but is also led as by the hand to find him...[It] is evident that man never attains to a true self-knowledge until he [has] previously contemplated the face of God, and come down after such contemplation to look into himself."[6]

John Calvin, *Institutes of the Christian Religion*

Community Discussion

1. What are various things people use to find a sense of identity?
2. What does it mean to find one's ultimate identity in Christ?
3. Why is understanding our identity crucial to spending our lives well?
4. What are the consequences of finding our identity in the wrong places?

+ **Grasping the Idea**

The Critical Journey[7]

The Christian life is a faith pilgrimage. As we progress in our spiritual journey, God shepherds us through various phases of faith formation. Contemplate the stages of spiritual progress in the timeline, thinking through where God might have you in your own journey.

Life of Discipleship

Learning about God toward strengthening our faith, we experience the joy of belonging to the Christian community and seek to get grounded in the essentials of the faith.

Recognition of God

Discovering God in humility, we experience awareness and awe of God and seek for deeper meaning by receiving the new life offered with faith in Christ.

Productive Life

Working for God, we express our uniqueness in the community and, feeling a sense of responsibility, we seek for ways to fulfill God's call on our lives using our gifts, setting goals, and making contributions to God's cause.

Life of Love

Reflecting on God, we experience a depth in our relationship with God and others where our focus is not simply on our productivity but on the union we enjoy with God and his people.

Journey Inward

Rediscovering God in restlessness, we experience a crisis of faith or loss of certainty and seek for life direction, personal renewal, and a revived vision of God.

Journey Outward

Surrendering to God, we allow God to transform us so that we go about God's calling for our lives with a genuine interest for other's well-being, an unhurried calmness, and a deep sense of God's acceptance.

Wall

Being confronted with what seems like an insurmountable impasse, we experience a deep reckoning of our true spiritual condition, allowing God to unmask us, and seek to yield to God's will and to rest in his unconditional love in greater surrender.

Discovering Your Design

Life Timeline

Take time to think through the timeline of your life.
Read through the following process and criteria and then chart out a
timeline that captures the overarching story of your life.

Contemplate
Think about the major movements of your life. Use the categories and criteria on the following page as a means to help you reflect on the various influences that have shaped your life.

Record
On the Life Timeline that follows, write down the various aspects that have been life-transforming. Move stage by stage up to the present day.

Observe
As you chronicle these formative moments, take note of patterns, themes, or insights that are beginning to become evident across the arc of your life. Document your impressions in the space below the timeline.

Label
Try to title each life phase with a word or phrase that captures the overall characteristics of that stage of your life.

Life Timeline Elements

**What Happened
in Each Phase**

Experiences
Highlights
Events
Roadblocks
Crises
Turning Points

**How You Grew
in Each Phase**

Growth
Education
Work
Family
Skills
Faith
Character
Achievements

**Who Impacted You
in Each Phase**

Relationships
Mentors
Friends
Family
Teachers
Church Leaders

**What You Learned
in Each Phase**

Wisdom
Ideas
Advice
Principles
Questions

Life Timeline

0–12
Childhood

31–55
Middle Adulthood

56–70
Later Adulthood

Impressions

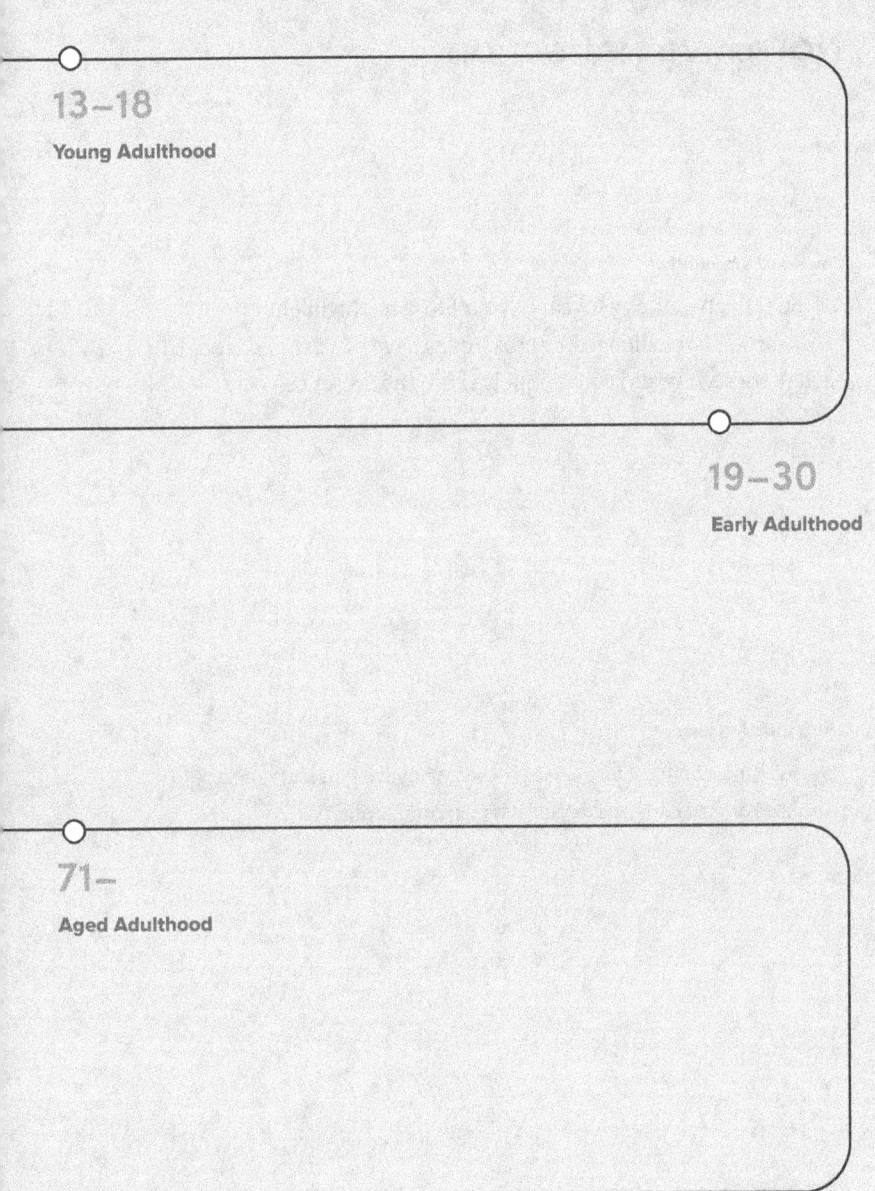

13–18
Young Adulthood

19–30
Early Adulthood

71–
Aged Adulthood

◿ **Chronicling the Journey**
Narrative Reflection

1

The Road Traveled

As you reflect on the past year of your life, what highlights, breakthroughs, challenges, or crossroads have you experienced? In each of these, how did you uniquely sense the presence of God?

2

The Inner Journey

As you think of where you are at today, what are you learning about the character of God and your own personal identity?

3

New Seasons

As you think of the year ahead, what transitions or new seasons do you sense God bringing you through? How can you prepare for the journey ahead?

SESSION TWO
2

Vocation

What am I called to do?

"You are the light of the world. A city set on a hill cannot be hidden. Nor do people light a lamp and put it under a basket, but on a stand, and it gives light to all in the house."

Matthew 5:14–15

"Every person, of every degree, state, sex, or condition without exception, must have some personal and particular calling to walk in." [8]

William Perkins, *A Treatise of the Vocations*

⚜ **Hearing the Word**

Uncovering Your Life's Work

²:¹ And you were dead in the trespasses and sins ² in which you once walked, following the course of this world, following the prince of the power of the air, the spirit that is now at work in the sons of disobedience— ³ among whom we all once lived in the passions of our flesh, carrying out the desires of the body and the mind, and were by nature children of wrath, like the rest of mankind. ⁴ But God, being rich in mercy, because of the great love with which he loved us, ⁵ even when we were dead in our trespasses, made us alive together with Christ—by grace you have been saved— ⁶ and raised us up with him and seated us with him in the heavenly places in Christ Jesus, ⁷ so that in the coming ages he might show the immeasurable riches of his grace in kindness toward us in Christ Jesus. ⁸ For by grace you have been saved through faith. And this is not your own doing; it is the gift of God, ⁹ not a result of works, so that no one may boast. ¹⁰ For we are his workmanship, created in Christ Jesus for good works, which God prepared beforehand, that we should walk in them.

¹¹ Therefore remember that at one time you Gentiles in the flesh, called "the uncircumcision" by what is called the circumcision, which is made in the flesh by hands— ¹² remember that you were at that time separated from Christ, alienated from the commonwealth of Israel and strangers to the covenants of promise, having no hope and without God in the world. ¹³ But now in Christ Jesus you who once were far off have been brought near by the blood of Christ. ¹⁴ For he himself is our peace, who has made us both one and has broken down in his flesh the dividing wall of hostility ¹⁵ by abolishing the law of commandments expressed in ordinances, that he might create in himself one new man in place of the two, so making peace, ¹⁶ and might reconcile us both to God in one body through the cross, thereby killing the hostility. ¹⁷ And he came and preached peace to you who were far off and peace to those who were near. ¹⁸ For through him we both have access in one Spirit to the Father. ¹⁹ So then you are no longer strangers and aliens, but you are fellow citizens with the saints and members of the household of God, ²⁰ built on the foundation of the apostles and prophets, Christ Jesus himself being the cornerstone, ²¹ in whom the whole structure, being joined together, grows into a holy temple in the Lord. ²² In him you also are being built together into a dwelling place for God by the Spirit.

Ephesians 2:1–22

Reflect

As a believer, how should you understand your vocation in Christ? Take some time to prayerfully read Ephesians 2:1–22 and then record your insights.

Seeking for Wisdom
Offering Ourselves to God in Our Work

"[We need] a thoroughgoing revolution in our whole attitude to work....[It] should be looked upon, not as a necessary drudgery to be undergone for the purpose of making money, but as a way of life in which the nature of man should find its proper exercise and delight and so fulfill itself to the glory of God...[Work is] a creative activity undertaken for the love of the work itself; and...man, made in God's image, should make things, as God makes them, for the sake of doing well a thing that is well worth doing....[Work] is not, primarily, a thing one does to live, but the thing one lives to do. It is, or it should be, the full expression of the worker's faculties, the thing in which he finds spiritual, mental and bodily satisfaction, and the medium in which he offers himself to God....It is the business of the Church to recognize that the secular vocation, as such, is sacred...When a man or woman is called to a particular job of secular work, that is as true a vocation as though he or she were called to specifically religious work....Let the Church remember this: that every maker and worker is called to serve God in his profession or trade—not outside of it....The only Christian work is good work well done. Let the Church see to it that the workers are Christian people and do their work well, as to God: then all the work will be Christian work, whether it is Church embroidery or sewage-farming....If work is to find its right place in the world, it is the duty of the Church to see to it that the work serves God, and that the worker serves the work."[9]

Dorothy L. Sayers, *"Why Work?"*

Explore

How do these quotes shape your understanding of your Christian vocation? After thoughtfully reading these quotes and exploring key ideas in community discussion, record your insights below.

Every Person Has His Strength

"Every man has, in the comprehensive sense of the term, his 'virtue' or strength (*virtus*). He cannot do many things which others do. But he can do something, perhaps quite a few things, which no one else can do, or do as he can. This is the personal aptitude in respect of which he is useful as none other. This, too, is part of his vocation, nor can it be without significance for his divine calling and his relation to it, his obedience to the command of God. Within its limit, but also in its fullness, he stands before God and has to listen and answer and obey. He did not choose it. He was not asked whether he is pleased with it. He has received it from God, his Creator and Lord, as he enters upon decision and act. It is thus, in his personal aptitude, that God has willed and created him, that He has caused him to be. This aptitude, too, can alter its form, at least in part. It can increase or decrease, expand or contract, become more sharp and specific or be blunted. Though he himself does not have full control over this, he may make some contribution. On the other hand, it has also its imperishable and distinctive characteristics which will persist in every change of form. He cannot escape from it, nor should he try to do so. He must not wish to jump out of his own skin. It is just as he is that he may come, when the command of God calls him, to meet the new thing which he is to be in the strength of this call. More and other than he is God does not require. This much however—himself in the personal aptitude with which he has been endowed—God does require. Hence in this respect, too, in and with faithfulness to God he is summoned to faithfulness to his vocation, to the confession of what he can do, and to its demonstration."[10]

Karl Barth, *"Vocation"*

Community Discussion

1. How do you understand the role of work in the Christian life?
2. How can you come to discover your particular gifting and calling?
3. What are the consequences of not walking in your God-given design?
4. What unique contribution do you think God has to make through you?

+ **Grasping the Idea**

Motivated Abilities Pattern[11]

Your motivations give clues to how God has hardwired you and they provide insight into your vocational purpose. Reflect on the various categories which make up your Motivated Abilities Pattern (MAP)—a helpful framework for discerning your God-given design—and see if you can identify how you best operate in each category. Evaluate whether your current life situation best maximizes your motivated abilities.

Motivated Abilities

the motivated abilities you naturally and instinctively use to accomplish anything that matters to you.

Subject Matter

the subject matter that you most naturally work on, with, or through.

Motivating Circumstances

the circumstances or environmental conditions in which you thrive.

Operating Relationships

the roles and relationships you prefer to have relative to others.

Primary Results

the central motivational thrust or "payoff" that drives your behavior.

Discovering Your Design

Life Inventory

In the following exercise, take inventory of your life. Your unique design is woven together with God's calling on your life. Think through the various aspects that make you uniquely you.

1. Contemplate

Think about the various categories that make up your unique, God-given design. Try to articulate these without over thinking them.

2. Record

Write down specific insights of how you were made. Try to identify the specific achievements, resources, gifts, passions, fulfillments, and motivations in your life.

3. Consult

Ask a trusted friend or mentor whether they agree with your observations. Have them adjust, comment, or record their own thoughts.

4. Reflect

Review whether your life situation maximizes how you are hardwired. Think about how you can better fulfill your vocation in your current situation, or what life changes would need to take place in order to more fully realize God's vision for your life.

Life Inventory Elements

Achievements **What Have You Done?**
Accomplishments, Exploits, Performances, Ventures

Resources **What Do You Have?**
Finances, Possessions, Networks, Relationships

Gifts **What Are You Good At?**
Skills, Talents, Abilities, Training, Expertise, Competencies

Passions **What Gets You Excited?**
Interests, Desires, Dreams, Future Visions

Fulfillments **What Gives You Satisfaction?**
Enjoyment, Pleasure, Contentment, Delight

Motivations **What Makes You Move?**
Ambitions, Aspirations, Recreations, Inspirations

Life Inventory

Achievements

Resources

Gifts

Passions

Fulfillments

Motivations

∠ **Chronicling the Journey**
Narrative Reflection

1
Achievements
What kind of past achievements can you remember that brought you a sense of satisfaction and fulfillment in life?

2
Passions
With what kinds of work or ministry are you most excited to be involved?

3
Motivations
What kind of vocational situations can you envision that would be most fulfilling? In other words, what would be the job description of your dream job?

SESSION THREE

Mission

Why am I here?

"In the same way, let your light shine before others, so that they may see your good works and give glory to your Father who is in heaven."

Matthew 5:16

"What God says is best, is best, though all the men in the world are against it." [12]

John Bunyan, *The Pilgrim's Progress*

Hearing the Word

Connecting Your Purpose to God's Mission

³¹ For this reason I, Paul, a prisoner of Christ Jesus on behalf of you Gentiles— ² assuming that you have heard of the stewardship of God's grace that was given to me for you, ³ how the mystery was made known to me by revelation, as I have written briefly. ⁴ When you read this, you can perceive my insight into the mystery of Christ, ⁵ which was not made known to the sons of men in other generations as it has now been revealed to his holy apostles and prophets by the Spirit. ⁶ This mystery is that the Gentiles are fellow heirs, members of the same body, and partakers of the promise in Christ Jesus through the gospel.

⁷ Of this gospel I was made a minister according to the gift of God's grace, which was given me by the working of his power. ⁸ To me, though I am the very least of all the saints, this grace was given, to preach to the Gentiles the unsearchable riches of Christ, ⁹ and to bring to light for everyone what is the plan of the mystery hidden for ages in God, who created all things, ¹⁰ so that through the church the manifold wisdom of God might now be made known to the rulers and authorities in the heavenly places. ¹¹ This was according to the eternal purpose that he has realized in Christ Jesus our Lord, ¹² in whom we have boldness and access with confidence through our faith in him. ¹³ So I ask you not to lose heart over what I am suffering for you, which is your glory.

¹⁴ For this reason I bow my knees before the Father, ¹⁵ from whom every family in heaven and on earth is named, ¹⁶ that according to the riches of his glory he may grant you to be strengthened with power through his Spirit in your inner being, ¹⁷ so that Christ may dwell in your hearts through faith—that you, being rooted and grounded in love, ¹⁸ may have strength to comprehend with all the saints what is the breadth and length and height and depth, ¹⁹ and to know the love of Christ that surpasses knowledge, that you may be filled with all the fullness of God. ²⁰ Now to him who is able to do far more abundantly than all that we ask or think, according to the power at work within us, ²¹ to him be glory in the church and in Christ Jesus throughout all generations, forever and ever. Amen.

Ephesians 3:1–21

Reflect

As a believer, what is the nature of your life purpose in Christ? Take some time to prayerfully read Ephesians 3:1–21 and then record your insights.

Seeking for Wisdom

Resolving to Live Our Lives for God's Glory

"Resolved, that *I will do whatsoever* I think to be most to God's glory and my own good, profit, and pleasure, on the whole: without any consideration of the time, whether now, or never so many myriads of ages hence;—to do whatever I think to be my *duty*, and most for the good and advantage of mankind in general,—whatever *difficulties* I meet with, how many and how great soever. Resolved, to be continually endeavouring to find some new *contrivance* to promote the forementioned things. Resolved, *never to do, be, or suffer* anything, in soul or body, less or more, but what tends to the glory of God. Resolved, never to lose one moment of *time*; but improve it in the most profitable way I possibly can. Resolved, to live with all my might, while I do live. Resolved, never to do anything which I should be afraid to do if it were the last hour of my life."[13]

Jonathan Edwards, *Resolutions*

Explore

How do these quotes shape your understanding of your Christian mission? After thoughtfully reading these quotes and exploring key ideas in community discussion, record your insights below.

Finding Joy in God's Mission

"There has been a long tradition which sees the mission of the Church primarily as obedience to a command. It has been customary to speak of 'the missionary mandate.' This way of putting the matter is certainly not without justification, and yet it seems to me that it misses the point. It tends to make mission a burden rather than a joy, to make it part of the law rather than part of the gospel. If one looks at the New Testament evidence one gets another impression. Mission begins with a kind of explosion of joy. The news that the rejected and crucified Jesus is alive is something that cannot possibly be suppressed. It must be told. Who could be silent about such a fact? The mission of the Church in the pages of the New Testament is more like the fallout from a vast explosion, a radioactive fallout which is not lethal but life-giving."[14]

Lesslie Newbigin, *The Gospel in a Pluralist Society*

Community Discussion

1. How do people try to find a sense of meaning in life?
2. How does Paul's understanding of his own life mission help us think about our purpose in life?
3. Why is it important to understand our mission in life? Why is it sometimes difficult to discern our life purpose?
4. What are the consequences of trying to live a life of meaning outside of God's purposes?

+ **Grasping the Idea**

The Great Commission[15]

We most realize our life purpose when it is aligned with God's revealed mission. Take a moment to reflect on this summary of the Great Commission. Meditate on how well your life is synchronized with God's purpose for his people.

"

"The Church is the pilgrim people of God.
It is on the move—hastening to the ends of the earth." [16]

Lesslie Newbigin, *The Household of God*

"World evangelization requires the whole church to take the whole gospel to the whole world." [17]

The Lausanne Covenant

"

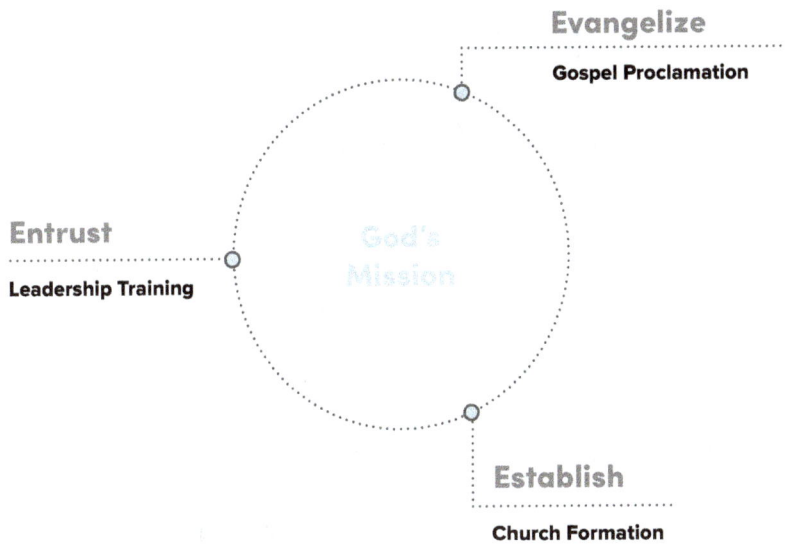

Great Commission
Matthew 28:16–20

ⁱ⁶ Now the eleven disciples went to Galilee, to the mountain to which Jesus had directed them. ¹⁷ And when they saw him they worshiped him, but some doubted. ¹⁸ And Jesus came and said to them, "All authority in heaven and on earth has been given to me. ¹⁹ Go therefore and **make disciples** of all nations, **baptizing** them in the name of the Father and of the Son and of the Holy Spirit, ²⁰ **teaching** them to observe all that I have commanded you. And behold, I am with you always, to the end of the age."

Pauline Cycle
Acts 14:21–23

²¹ When they had **preached the gospel** to that city and had ***made many disciples***, they returned to Lystra and to Iconium and to Antioch, ²² **strengthening the souls of the disciples, encouraging them to continue in the faith**, and saying that through many tribulations we must enter the kingdom of God. ²³ And when they had **appointed elders** for them in every church, with prayer and fasting they committed them to the Lord in whom they had believed.

Discovering Your Design

Life Purpose

Take time to contemplate the purpose of your life. Read through the steps below and then seek to write out your purpose in each sphere of your life.

1. Review
Review elements from your Life Inventory (achievements, resources, gifts, passions, fulfillments, and motivations). Think about how each connects with various spheres of your life: individual, family, church, and world. Record these insights in the appropriate circle.

2. Reflect
Consider the unique contribution God would have you to make in each of these life spheres. Meditate on life purposes that resonate with your own passions and gifts along with God's overall purposes for His world.

3. Write
Write out a complete sentence that captures your purpose in each sphere of life: individual, family, church, and world.

4. Synthesize
Seek to capture your specific God-given purpose in life by writing one unique, overall mission statement for your life.

Life Purpose Elements

Individual Purpose — What is God calling you to in your personal life?

Family Purpose — What is God calling you to in your immediate relations and closest relationships?

Church Purpose — What is God calling you to in your church community?

World Purpose — What is God calling you to in your neighborhood, immediate locale, and surrounding world?

Unique Purpose Statement — Overall, what is the unique mission of your life?

Life Purpose

Individual Insights

Family Insights

Church Insights

World Insights

Individual Purpose Statement

Family Purpose Statement

Church Purpose Statement

World Purpose Statement

Unique Purpose Statement

Chronicling the Journey
Narrative Reflection

1

Family Member
How are you fulfilling your life mission in the context of your family?

2

Community Participant
How are you living out God's purpose in the context of the church community?

3

World Citizen
How are you living out God's mission in the world?

SESSION FOUR
4

Community

Where do I belong?

"So whatever you wish that others would do to you, do also to them, for this is the Law and the Prophets."

Matthew 7:12

"No man is an island entire of itself. Every man is a piece of the continent, a part of the main." [18]

John Donne, *Devotions*

⚿ **Hearing the Word**

Finding a Place to Belong

⁴:¹ I therefore, a prisoner for the Lord, urge you to walk in a manner worthy of the calling to which you have been called, ² with all humility and gentleness, with patience, bearing with one another in love, ³ eager to maintain the unity of the Spirit in the bond of peace. ⁴ There is one body and one Spirit—just as you were called to the one hope that belongs to your call— ⁵ one Lord, one faith, one baptism, ⁶ one God and Father of all, who is over all and through all and in all. ⁷ But grace was given to each one of us according to the measure of Christ's gift. ⁸ Therefore it says, "When he ascended on high he led a host of captives, and he gave gifts to men."

⁹ (In saying, "He ascended," what does it mean but that he had also descended into the lower regions, the earth? ¹⁰ He who descended is the one who also ascended far above all the heavens, that he might fill all things.) ¹¹ And he gave the apostles, the prophets, the evangelists, the shepherds and teachers, ¹² to equip the saints for the work of ministry, for building up the body of Christ, ¹³ until we all attain to the unity of the faith and of the knowledge of the Son of God, to mature manhood, to the measure of the stature of the fullness of Christ, ¹⁴ so that we may no longer be children, tossed to and fro by the waves and carried about by every wind of doctrine, by human cunning, by craftiness in deceitful schemes. ¹⁵ Rather, speaking the truth in love, we are to grow up in every way into him who is the head, into Christ, ¹⁶ from whom the whole body, joined and held together by every joint with which it is equipped, when each part is working properly, makes the body grow so that it builds itself up in love.

¹⁷ Now this I say and testify in the Lord, that you must no longer walk as the Gentiles do, in the futility of their minds. ¹⁸ They are darkened in their understanding, alienated from the life of God because of the ignorance that is in them, due to their hardness of heart. ¹⁹ They have become callous and have given themselves up to sensuality, greedy to practice every kind of impurity. ²⁰ But that is not the way you learned Christ!— ²¹ assuming that you have heard about him and were taught in him, as the truth is in Jesus, ²² to put off your old self, which belongs to your former manner of life and is corrupt through deceitful desires, ²³ and to be renewed in the spirit of your minds, ²⁴ and to put on the new self, created after the likeness of God in true righteousness and holiness. ²⁵ Therefore, having put away falsehood, let each one of you speak the truth with his neighbor, for we are members one of another. ²⁶ Be angry and do not sin; do not let the sun go down on your anger, ²⁷ and give no opportunity to the devil. ²⁸ Let the thief no longer steal, but rather let him labor, doing honest work with his own hands, so that he may have something to share with anyone in need. ²⁹ Let no corrupting talk come out of your mouths, but only such as is good for building up, as fits the occasion, that it may give grace to those who hear. ³⁰ And do not grieve the Holy Spirit of God, by whom you were sealed for the day of redemption. ³¹ Let all bitterness and wrath and anger and clamor and slander be put away from you, along with all malice. ³² Be kind to one another, tenderhearted, forgiving one another, as God in Christ forgave you.

Ephesians 4:1–32

Reflect

As a believer, what is the nature of community in Christ? Take some time to prayerfully read Ephesians 4:1–32 and then record your insights.

Seeking for Wisdom

Enjoying Genuine Christian Community

"Whoever cannot be alone should beware of community. Such people will only do harm to themselves and to the community. Alone you stood before God when God called you. Alone you had to obey God's voice. Alone you had to take up your cross, struggle, and pray and alone you will die and give an account to God. You cannot avoid yourself, for it is precisely God who has singled you out. If you do not want to be alone, you are rejecting Christ's call to you, and you can have no part in the community of those who are called....But the reverse is also true. Whoever cannot stand being in community should beware of being alone. You are called into the community of faith; the call was not meant for you alone. You carry your cross, you struggle, and you pray in the community of faith, the community of those who are called. You are not alone even when you die, and on the day of judgment you will be only one member of the great community of faith of Jesus Christ. If you neglect the community of other Christians, you reject the call of Jesus Christ, and thus your being alone can only become harmful for you....We recognize, then, that only as we stand within the community can we be alone, and only those who are alone can live in the community. Both belong together. Only in the community do we learn to be properly alone; and only in being alone do we learn to live properly in the community....Each taken by itself has profound pitfalls and perils. Those who want community without solitude plunge into the void of words and feelings, and those who seek solitude without community perish in the bottomless pit of vanity, self-infatuation, and despair. Whoever cannot be alone should beware of community. Whoever cannot stand being in community should beware of being alone."[19]

Dietrich Bonhoeffer, *Life Together*

Explore

How do these quotes give definition to your understanding of Christian community? After thoughtfully reading these quotes and exploring key ideas in community discussion, record your insights below.

Finding the Faithfulness of True Friendship

"Friendship seems as necessary an element of a comfortable existence in this world as fire or water, or even air itself...He who would be happy here must have friends; and he who would be happy hereafter, must, above all things, find a friend in the world to come, in the person of God, the Father of his people....Friendship, however, though very pleasing and exceedingly blessed, has been the cause of the greatest misery to men when it has been unworthy and unfaithful; for just in proportion as a good friend is sweet, a false friend is full of bitterness... Fidelity is an absolute necessary in a true friend; we cannot rejoice in men unless they will stand faithful to us....Faithfulness to us in our faults is a certain sign of fidelity in a friend. You may depend upon that man who will tell you of your faults in a kind and considerate manner. Fawning hypocrites, insidious flatterers, are the sweepings and offal of friendship. They are but the parasites upon that noble tree. But true friends put enough trust in you to tell you openly of your faults. Give me for a friend the man who will speak honestly of me before my face; who will not tell first one neighbor, and then another, but who will come straight to my house, and say, 'Sir, I feel there is such-and-such a thing in you, which, as my brother, I must tell you of.' That man is a true friend; he has proved himself to be so."[20]

Charles Spurgeon, "A Faithful Friend"

Community Discussion

1. When can you ever remember being part of a meaningful relationship or community? What made these relationships so impactful?

2. Why is Christian community important for our growth as a disciple of Christ?

3. What are obstacles that challenge deep relationships and community life?

4. How can you more significantly prioritize fellowship with your church community?

+ **Grasping the Idea**

Mentoring Functions[21]

Strong Christian community requires strong mentoring relationships (cf. Titus 2). Contemplate the possible types of mentors and the unique role each plays in your own formation. Consider how you might cultivate a diverse mentoring network in your life.

Discipler	A mature follower of Christ who establishes others in the essentials of the Christian faith.
Spiritual Guide	A wise overseer who provides accountability, insight, and instruction in making spiritual progress.
Coach	A competent trainer with expertise to habituate a disciple in the use of spiritual skills.
Counselor	A discerning confidant who offers timely advice and wise perspective on personal and ministry issues.
Teacher	A knowledgeable instructor who imparts understanding and enlightenment to relevant concerns.
Sponsor	A faithful patron who extends context-specific direction and ongoing support in vocational progress.
Contemporary Model	A present-day exemplar who embodies a life and ministry worthy of emulation.
Historical Ideal	A notable figure in history who has led a compelling and imitable life and ministry.
Divine Contact	A timely placed individual who serves as God's representative to convey necessary wisdom for pressing issues of the present time.

Active — Discipler

Active — Spiritual Guide

Active — Coach

Occasional — Counselor

Occasional — Teacher

Occasional — Sponsor

Passive — Contemporary Model

Passive — Historical Ideal

Passive — Divine Contact

Discovering Your Design

Life Mentoring

A decade-based mentoring exercise helps us diversify our web of relationships. Try to identify life mentors from various decades of life and from various spheres of life. Be sure to identify mentors that will pour into your life and those whom you will mentor yourself.

Ponder

Reflect on the areas of your life where you need wisdom. Consider areas where you are encountering problems, major choices, gripping strongholds, or maturity gaps.

Invest

Select various people in each decade of life with whom you could connect to gain wisdom in these specific areas of life. Focus on identifying mentors older than you. Also, consider those who might serve as mentors in your own decade as well as those who are younger than you. Do not feel pressure to find one mentor who can address all life issues.

Identify

Consider individuals in which God is calling you to invest. Typically these individuals will be in decades younger than you but do not need to be exclusively so.

Plan

Come up with a plan to reach out to these mentors and mentees, thinking through appropriate frequencies and venues.

Life Mentoring Elements

Mentors	Those who can speak wisdom into specific areas of your life.
Mentees	Those to whom you can speak wisdom and offer guidance.
Potential Subject Areas	Christian Maturity Finances Leadership Sexual Purity Relationships Parenting Physical Health Interpersonal Conflict Retirement Politics Marriage Family Life Home Improvement Investments Employment/Vocation Education Theology Ministry

Life Mentoring

	Name	Subject and Plan
0–10		
10–20		
20–30		
30–40		

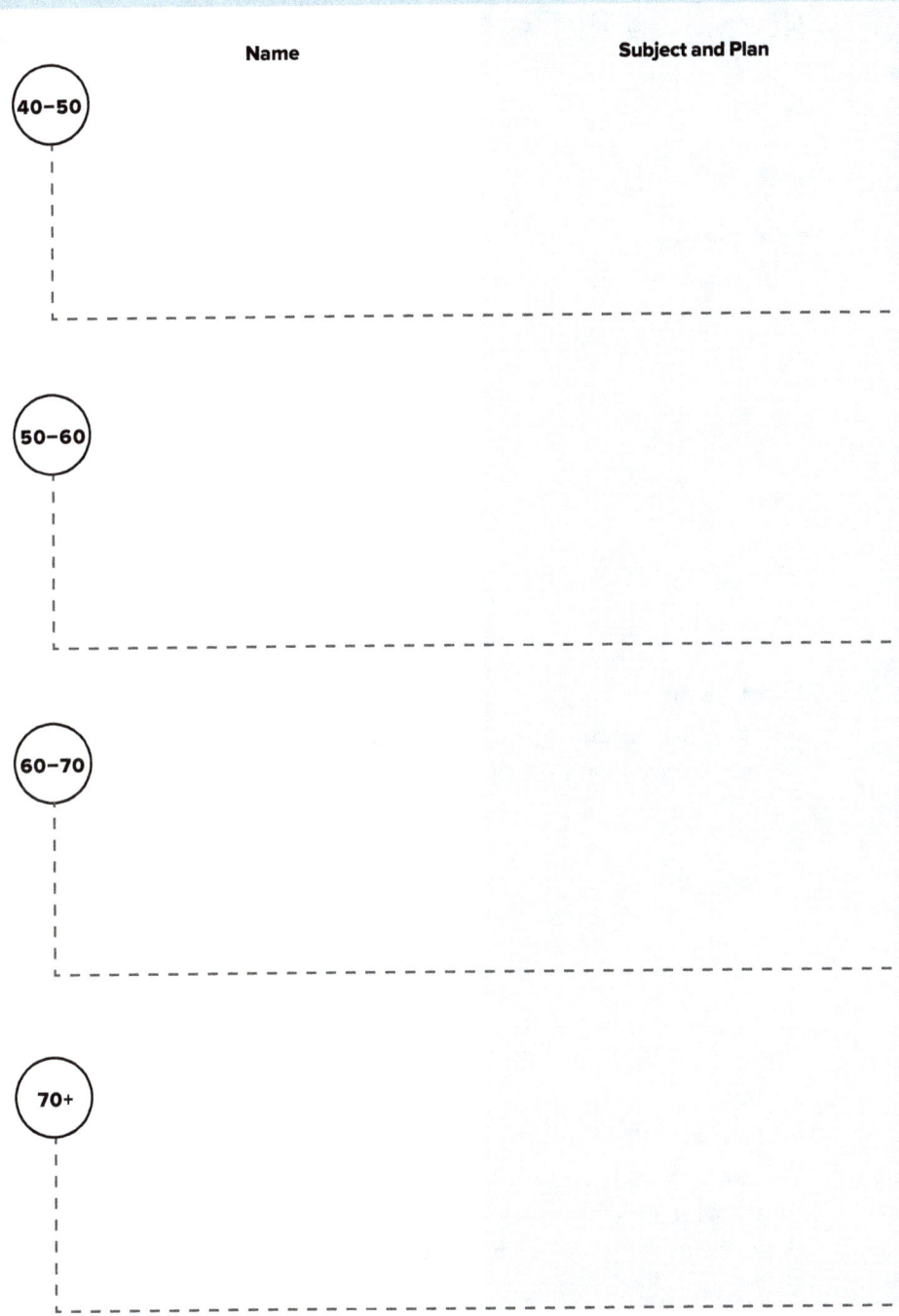

∠ **Chronicling the Journey**

Narrative Reflection

1
Cloud of Witnesses
What past mentors have made a mark on your life?

2
Current Investments
In what current relationships are you making an investment? How are you investing in them? Who is currently investing in you?

3
Next Steps
What are the next kinds of relationships that you need to form and invest in for your own personal development and for the development of the church community?

SESSION FIVE
5

Values

Which things are of greatest importance?

"For where your treasure is, there your heart will be also."

Matthew 6:21

"Whatever your heart clings to and confides in, that is really your God." [22]

Martin Luther, *Large Catechism*

Hearing the Word

Walking in God's Priorities

^{5:1} Therefore be imitators of God, as beloved children. ² And walk in love, as Christ loved us and gave himself up for us, a fragrant offering and sacrifice to God. ³ But sexual immorality and all impurity or covetousness must not even be named among you, as is proper among saints. ⁴ Let there be no filthiness nor foolish talk nor crude joking, which are out of place, but instead let there be thanksgiving. ⁵ For you may be sure of this, that everyone who is sexually immoral or impure, or who is covetous (that is, an idolater), has no inheritance in the kingdom of Christ and God. ⁶ Let no one deceive you with empty words, for because of these things the wrath of God comes upon the sons of disobedience. ⁷ Therefore do not become partners with them; ⁸ for at one time you were darkness, but now you are light in the Lord. Walk as children of light ⁹ (for the fruit of light is found in all that is good and right and true), ¹⁰ and try to discern what is pleasing to the Lord. ¹¹ Take no part in the unfruitful works of darkness, but instead expose them. ¹² For it is shameful even to speak of the things that they do in secret. ¹³ But when anything is exposed by the light, it becomes visible, ¹⁴ for anything that becomes visible is light. Therefore it says, "Awake, O sleeper, and arise from the dead, and Christ will shine on you."

¹⁵ Look carefully then how you walk, not as unwise but as wise, ¹⁶ making the best use of the time, because the days are evil. ¹⁷ Therefore do not be foolish, but understand what the will of the Lord is. ¹⁸ And do not get drunk with wine, for that is debauchery, but be filled with the Spirit, ¹⁹ addressing one another in psalms and hymns and spiritual songs, singing and making melody to the Lord with your heart, ²⁰ giving thanks always and for everything to God the Father in the name of our Lord Jesus Christ, ²¹ submitting to one another out of reverence for Christ.

Ephesians 5:1–21

Reflect

As a believer, what gives shape to godly priorities in Christ? Take some time to prayerfully read Ephesians 5:1–21 and then record your insights.

Seeking for Wisdom

Improving How We Spend Our Time

"You are accountable to God for your time. Time is a talent given us by God; he hath set us our day; and it is not for nothing. Our day was appointed for some work; therefore he will, at the day's end, call us to an account. We must give account to him of the improvement of all our time. We are God's servants; as a servant is accountable to his master, how he spends his time when he is sent forth to work, so are we accountable to God. If men would aright consider this, and keep it in mind, would they not improve their time otherwise than they do? Would you not behave otherwise than you do, if you considered with yourselves every morning, that you must give an account to God, how you shall have spent that day? And if you considered with yourselves, at the beginning of every evening, that you must give an account to God, how you shall have spent that evening? Christ hath told us, that for every idle word which men speak they shall give account in the day of judgment... How well, therefore, may we conclude, that we must give an account of all our idle misspent time!"[23]

Jonathan Edwards, *"The Preciousness of Time"*

Explore

How do these quotes shape your understanding of your Christian values? After thoughtfully reading these quotes and exploring key ideas in community discussion, record your insights below.

Danger of Diversion

"If our condition were truly happy, we would not need diversion from thinking of it in order to make ourselves happy....The only thing which consoles us for our miseries is diversion, and yet this is the greatest of our miseries. For it is this which principally hinders us from reflecting upon ourselves, and which makes us insensibly ruin ourselves. Without this we should be in a state of weariness, and this weariness would spur us to seek a more solid means of escaping from it. But diversion amuses us, and leads us unconsciously to death....We do not rest satisfied with the present. We anticipate the future as too slow in coming, as if in order to hasten its course; or we recall the past, to stop its too rapid flight. So imprudent are we that we wander in the times which are not ours, and do not think of the only one which belongs to us; and so idle are we that we dream of those times which are no more, and thoughtlessly overlook that which alone exists. For the present is generally painful to us. We conceal it from out sight, because it troubles us; and if it be delightful to us, we regret to see it pass away. We try to sustain it by the future, and think of arranging matters which are not in our power, for a time which we have no certainty of reaching.... Let each one examine his thoughts, and he will find them all occupied with the past and the future. We scarcely ever think of the present; and if we think of it, it is only to take light from it to arrange the future. The present is never our end. The past and the present are our means; the future alone is our end. So we never live, but we hope to live; and, as we are always preparing to be happy, it is inevitable we should never be so."[24]

Blaise Pascal, *Pensées*

Community Discussion

1. How would you describe the current priorities that are shaping your life?
2. How should a believer determine his or her life priorities?
3. What are some of the competing forces that distract us from godly priorities?
4. How can you shape your life goals around God's priorities?

+ **Grasping the Idea**

Six Great Ideas[25]

The things we prize and cherish determine our values—that which we consider most important in life. As we consider our values and the goals shaped by them, reflect on these six fundamental ideas as a substructure for life and reality. Consider how these values would help you set your own personal priorities in life.

The ideas we judge by.

Truth
Believing what is real.

Goodness
Treasuring what is virtuous.

Beauty
Celebrating what is majestic.

The ideas we act on.

Liberty
Seeking
what is free.

Equality
Embracing what is
noble.

Justice
Upholding what
is righteous.

Discovering Your Design

Life Goals

Envision specific goals for your life that would synchronize with God's priorities. Consider goals at a one year, five year, and lifetime range. Moreover, categorize your goals as they relate to personal development, family maturity, church contribution, and world impact. Fill out the charts on the following pages with specific goals for each of these major categories. Do not feel the need to be exhaustive, but strive to be as specific as possible. Prayerfully consider what goals God is calling you to pursue. Seek to identify at least one major goal in each of the four major areas of your life.

1
Envision
Anticipate what God is calling you to as you consider one year, five year, and lifetime goals.

2
Meditate
In each of these time frames, contemplate specific goals in the four major spheres of your life: individual, family, church, and world.

3
Record
List the specific goals you believe God is calling you to focus for each life sphere and each span of time.

4
Evaluate
Review your progress on these goals throughout the year, making future plans for things you want to work on in your personal development.

Life Goal Elements

Individual Physical, Emotional, Relational, Spiritual, Educational

Family Parental, Marital, Sibling, Financial, Extended Family

Church Service, Stewardship, Mentorship, Community, Ministry, Leadership

World Vocation, Neighborhood, Society, Politics

Life Goals

	Individual	Family
1 Year		
5 Year		
Lifetime		

Church　　　　　　　　　**World**

∠ **Chronicling the Journey**

Narrative Reflection

1

Future Forecast

As you envision your life in the years ahead, what picture would you be excited to see?

2

Potential Hindrances

What potential obstacles can you envision which would hinder your pursuit and accomplishment of these goals?

3

Course Correction

What kind of adjustments would you need to make in order to accomplish this vision of your life?

Habits

How will I move forward?

"Everyone then who hears these words of mine and does them will be like a wise man who built his house on the rock."

Matthew 7:24

"It is vanity to wish for length of life, and to care little that the life should be well spent." [26]

Thomas à Kempis, *The Imitation of Christ*

⚤ **Hearing the Word**

Preparing for Life's Battles

5:22 Wives, submit to your own husbands, as to the Lord. 23 For the husband is the head of the wife even as Christ is the head of the church, his body, and is himself its Savior. 24 Now as the church submits to Christ, so also wives should submit in everything to their husbands. 25 Husbands, love your wives, as Christ loved the church and gave himself up for her, 26 that he might sanctify her, having cleansed her by the washing of water with the word, 27 so that he might present the church to himself in splendor, without spot or wrinkle or any such thing, that she might be holy and without blemish. 28 In the same way husbands should love their wives as their own bodies. He who loves his wife loves himself. 29 For no one ever hated his own flesh, but nourishes and cherishes it, just as Christ does the church, 30 because we are members of his body. 31 "Therefore a man shall leave his father and mother and hold fast to his wife, and the two shall become one flesh." 32 This mystery is profound, and I am saying that it refers to Christ and the church. 33 However, let each one of you love his wife as himself, and let the wife see that she respects her husband. 6:1 Children, obey your parents in the Lord, for this is right. 2 "Honor your father and mother" (this is the first commandment with a promise), 3 "that it may go well with you and that you may live long in the land." 4 Fathers, do not provoke your children to anger, but bring them up in the discipline and instruction of the Lord. 5 Bondservants, obey your earthly masters with fear and trembling, with a sincere heart, as you would Christ, 6 not by the way of eye-service, as people-pleasers, but as bondservants of Christ, doing the will of God from the heart, 7 rendering service with a good will as to the Lord and not to man, 8 knowing that whatever good anyone does, this he will receive back from the Lord, whether he is a bondservant or is free. 9 Masters, do the same to them, and stop your threatening, knowing that he who is both their Master and yours is in heaven, and that there is no partiality with him.

10 Finally, be strong in the Lord and in the strength of his might. 11 Put on the whole armor of God, that you may be able to stand against the schemes of the devil. 12 For we do not wrestle against flesh and blood, but against the rulers, against the authorities, against the cosmic powers over this present darkness, against the spiritual forces of evil in the heavenly places. 13 Therefore take up the whole armor of God, that you may be able to withstand in the evil day, and having done all, to stand firm. 14 Stand therefore, having fastened on the belt of truth, and having put on the breastplate of righteousness, 15 and, as shoes for your feet, having put on the readiness given by the gospel of peace. 16 In all circumstances take up the shield of faith, with which you can extinguish all the flaming darts of the evil one; 17 and take the helmet of salvation, and the sword of the Spirit, which is the word of God, 18 praying at all times in the Spirit, with all prayer and supplication. To that end, keep alert with all perseverance, making supplication for all the saints, 19 and also for me, that words may be given to me in opening my mouth boldly to proclaim the mystery of the gospel, 20 for which I am an ambassador in chains, that I may declare it boldly, as I ought to speak.

21 So that you also may know how I am and what I am doing, Tychicus the beloved brother and faithful minister in the Lord will tell you everything. 22 I have sent him to you for this very purpose, that you may know how we are, and that he may encourage your hearts. 23 Peace be to the brothers, and love with faith, from God the Father and the Lord Jesus Christ. 24 Grace be with all who love our Lord Jesus Christ with love incorruptible.

Ephesians 5:22–6:24

Reflect

As a believer, how should you think of godly habits in Christ? Take some time to prayerfully read Ephesians 5:22–6:24 and then record your insights.

∧∧ **Seeking for Wisdom**

Surrendering Ourselves Without Reserve

"We need to be in a position of entire consecration, utterly and absolutely at the disposal of our Lord. We do not need a larger number than He has brought together; we do not need greater ability; we do no need wider experience, in order to have full blessing; but we do need to be near to our Lord, very near to Him; to have him reigning in our hearts. We want that He should know, and to know ourselves, that all we have and all we are in unreserved consecration given up to Him... Oh, let us every day seek to be all for Jesus; and being all for Jesus, we shall be all for one another, and all drawn together. Let us just give up our work, our thoughts, our plans, ourselves, our lives, our loved ones, our influence, our all, right into His hand, and then when we have given all over to Him there will be nothing left for us to be troubled about or to make trouble about; when all is in His hand all will be safe, and all be wisely dealt with, all will be done and well done. When the eye is single, when the heart is true to Christ, then and then alone the whole body will be full of light...How shall we get it? Simply by unreserved surrender, taking our Lord as King, and putting ourselves and all we have and all we are in His hands."[27]

J. Hudson Taylor, *"Sermon on Matthew 15:29–38"*

Explore

How do these quotes shape your understanding of your Christian habits? After thoughtfully reading these quotes and exploring key ideas in community discussion, record your insights below.

Giving Ourselves to God's Command

"The totality of the believer's response is discipline...We might say the discipline is the disciple's 'career.' It defines the very shape of the disciple's life...Discipline is the believer's answer to God's call. It is the recognition, not of the solution to his problems or the supply of his needs, but of mastery. God addresses us. We are responsible—that is, we must make a response....Discipline is the wholehearted yes to the call of God. When I know myself called, summoned, addressed, taken possession of, known, acted upon, I have heard the Master. I put myself gladly, fully, and forever at His disposal, and to whatever He says my answer is yes....Christian discipline means placing oneself under orders. It is no mere business of self-improvement, to be listed along with speed-reading, weight watching, jogging, time management, home repairs, or how to win friends....The disciple is one who has made a very simple decision. Jesus invites us to follow Him, and the disciple accepts the invitation....Any 'soldier,' any candidate for Christian discipline, ought daily to report to his commanding officer for duty. At your service, Lord....Jesus Christ is Savior because he is Lord. He is Lord because He is Savior. I cannot be saved from my sins unless I am also saved from myself, so Christ must be 'commanding officer' in my life."[28]

Elizabeth Elliot, *Discipline*

Community Discussion

1. In what ways can the life of faith be compared to a battle?
2. What are different spheres of life in which we seek to live out our Christian faith?
3. What kinds of habits help us engage our Christian life as a spiritual battle?
4. What would it look like to intentionally organize your life around godly habits and rhythms?

+ Grasping the Idea

The Spirit of the Disciplines[29]

Throughout the history of the Christian faith, disciples have outfitted themselves with spiritual disciplines. Survey these basic faith practices. Note that certain habits are disciplines of *abstinence* (things from which we refrain) and others are disciplines of *engagement* (things to which we give ourselves). Ponder how you might incorporate these disciplines into your regular rhythms of life.

Disciplines of Abstinence

Sabbath
Pausing from work for rest and worship.

Sacrifice
Forsaking things we rely upon to entirely trust God.

Solitude
Refraining from interaction with others.

Secrecy
Concealing good works from recognition.

Silence
Keeping ourselves from noise and sound.

Chastity
Rejecting immoral or impure influences and actions.

Frugality
Living simply by only purchasing what is necessary.

Fasting
Abstaining from eating or drinking (or some other life comfort) for a period of time.

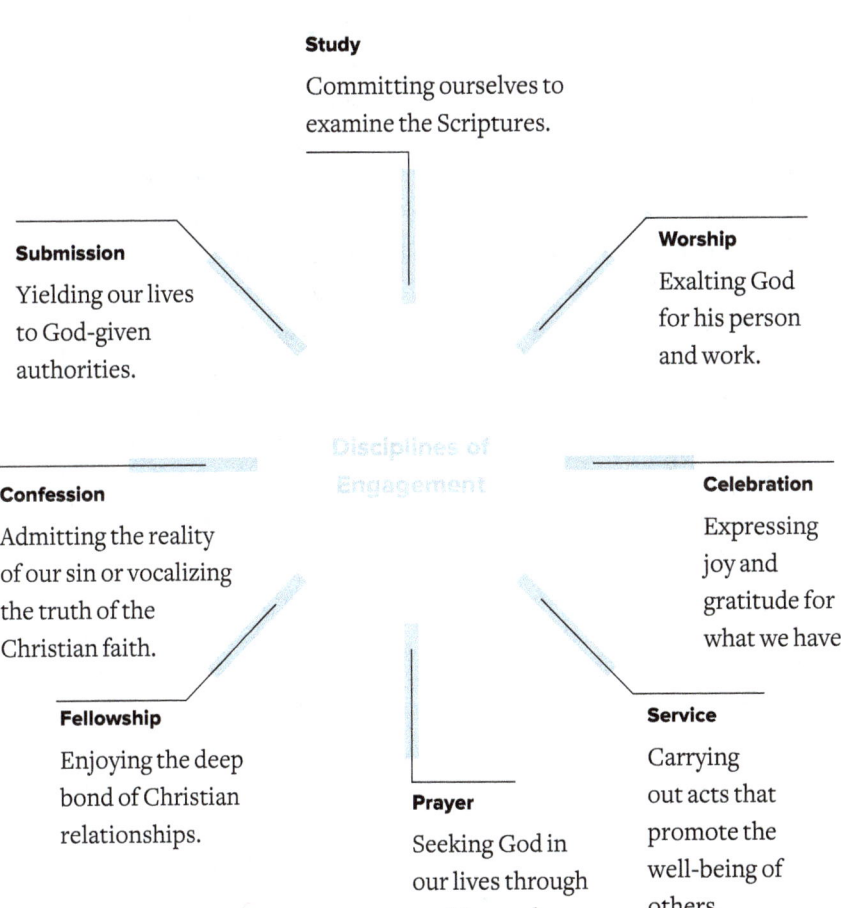

Study
Committing ourselves to examine the Scriptures.

Submission
Yielding our lives to God-given authorities.

Worship
Exalting God for his person and work.

Disciplines of Engagement

Confession
Admitting the reality of our sin or vocalizing the truth of the Christian faith.

Celebration
Expressing joy and gratitude for what we have.

Fellowship
Enjoying the deep bond of Christian relationships.

Prayer
Seeking God in our lives through petition and intercession.

Service
Carrying out acts that promote the well-being of others.

Discovering Your Design

Life Habits

If we want to put on the whole armor of God, being intentional with our time is crucial. Design a weekly schedule that identifies the major rhythms of your life, incorporates all areas of your life (individual, marriage, parenting, education, relationships, work, finances, etc.), builds valuable habits, and reflects your overall goals in the upcoming year. Feel free to adjust the schedule throughout the year.

1
Evaluate
Review how you currently spend your time on a weekly basis. Identify misplaced priorities that need to be removed as well as priorities that have been neglected but need to be added to your life.

2
Reflect
Think about how to best incorporate these priorities in your life. Seek to identify rhythms, habits, and goals that can be incorporated in the daily, weekly, monthly, quarterly, and yearly rhythms of your life.

3
Schedule
Outline these rhythms in the weekly calendar in a way that gives emphasis to your life priorities. Try to identify blocks of time that you can consistently commit to these habits.

4
Review
Revisit your calendar on a regular basis throughout the year and modify any rhythms that need to be adjusted.

Life Habit Elements

Personal Disciplines	Prayer, Fasting, Scripture Reading, Silence, Lectio Divina, Daily Examen
Vocational Responsibilities	Meetings, Communications, Projects, Daily Tasks
Family Rhythms	Family Worship (Scripture Reading, Singing, Testimony, Memorization, Catechism), Regular Activities, Relationship Building
Church Participation	Mentoring Connections, Prayer, Mutual Encouragement, Ministry Responsibilities
World Engagement	Neighbor Connections, Evangelism Outreach, Prayer Walking, City Welfare, Civic Involvement, Public Life, Community Participation

Life Habits

M

T

W

T

F

S   S

∠ **Chronicling the Journey**

Narrative Reflection

1

One Year Ago

How well did you fulfill your plans from the previous year? What progress have you made?

2

The Present Moment

How are you feeling about coming up with an intentional plan for your life?

3

One Year Later

What would make you excited to hear about yourself if you could paint a picture of your progress one year later?

Seasonal Review

Keeping Log of Personal Progress

....

This second movement of the journal is a **Seasonal Review**. Serving as a periodic assessment throughout the year, this section offers space for personal inventory, progress reports, growth plans, church community feedback, and peer encouragement. Set to a quarterly rhythm, each seasonal review is performed best in the context of a mentoring relationship and committed community which is invested in your ongoing formation. Therefore, while you should take personal time to prayerfully appraise your spiritual health, also make sure to invite mentors and church community members to give their personal feedback on your spiritual progress.

How to use

Personal Inventory

The following inventory offers questions for self-examination rooted in the Pastoral Epistles (1–2 Timothy and Titus). Reflectively answer each of the following questions as a means to assess your spiritual health. On the scale of 1–5, 1 represents an area of significant struggle and 5 represents an area of spiritual maturity. In your mentor and/or church community meetings, share your assessment to receive honest and loving perspective on your maturity.

Progress Report

As you reflect on your previous months of growth and also consider future months, answer the assessment questions as a means to review your past quarter and to anticipate the upcoming quarter. Debrief with your mentor and/or church community in celebration, confession, and anticipation.

Community Feedback

As you engage in mentor and/or church community meetings, use this space to capture their words of encouragement, loving exhortations, noteworthy observations, and specific insights about your spiritual maturity. Record feedback from spiritual advisers, trusted friends, and church community members about your growth in the past season. Feel free to capture these insights yourself or to have these trusted confidants directly record their own thoughts in the journal.

Growth Plan

Reflect on your personal inventory and progress report with your trusted mentor and identify areas of life that you want to intentionally work on. Consider the biblical rationale for your chosen areas. Together with the wisdom of your mentor, come up with a concrete plan to pursue growth in your goals. Toward the end of the season, assess your progress.

Time Period: _____

Seasonal Review
Quarter 1

The following pages outline a pathway for your **first** seasonal review of the year. This series of exercises is meant to give you some space to appraise your progress over the past quarter as well as envision a plan for the upcoming months. Take time for this life audit by completing the personal inventory, summarizing a progress report, seeking mentor feedback, and composing a growth plan. Try to make this both a personal time as well as a time where key mentors and those in your church community are invited into the reflection and planning process.

Identity

Conversion

How apparent is your conversion to the faith as one who has come to "believe in [Jesus] for eternal life" (1 Tim 1:16), being able to confess "that Christ Jesus came into the world to save sinners, of whom I am the foremost" (1 Tim 1:15)?

① ② ③ ④ ⑤

Comments

Character

How evidently are you embodying a holy life that is "above reproach" (1 Tim 3:2) by fleeing all godlessness to "pursue righteousness, godliness, faith, love, steadfastness, gentleness" (1 Tim 6:11)?

① ② ③ ④ ⑤

Comments

Progress

How dutifully are you giving yourself to your own faith formation in practice, devotion, and persistence "so that all may see your progress" (1 Tim 4:15)?

① ② ③ ④ ⑤

Comments

Approval

How concerned are you ultimately about God's opinion of you in all things (not the opinions of men) that you "do your best to present yourself to God as one approved" (2 Tim 2:15)?

① ② ③ ④ ⑤

Comments

Emotions

How maturely do you live out of healthy emotions, taking confidence that "God gave us a spirit not of fear but of power and love and self-control" (2 Tim 1:7)?

① ② ③ ④ ⑤

Comments

Vocation

Self-Awareness/Giftedness

How aware are you of God's calling on your life to "fulfill your ministry" (2 Tim 4:5), being careful to not "neglect the gift you have" (1 Tim 4:14) but rather "to fan into flame the gift of God" (2 Tim 1:6) which has been given to you?

① ② ③ ④ ⑤

Comments

Skills

How competent are you becoming in your life and ministry skills, doing "your best to present yourself to God as one approved, a worker who has no need to be ashamed, rightly handling the word of truth" (2 Tim 2:15)?

① ② ③ ④ ⑤

Comments

Resources

How responsibly are you using your resources toward an eternal investment to "be rich in good works" and "generous and ready to share," not setting "hopes on the uncertainty of riches, but on God, who richly provides us with everything to enjoy" (1 Tim 6:17–18)?

① ② ③ ④ ⑤

Comments

Work

How conscientious are you in your vocation, performing it as a ministry toward God as would a hard-working farmer, fully devoted athlete, and duty-bound soldier (2 Tim 2:3–7)?

① ② ③ ④ ⑤

Comments

Motivations

How sincerely are your motivations coming from a "pure heart" (1 Tim 1:5), receiving God's good gifts "with thanksgiving," (1 Tim 4:4) not being given to insincerity, deception, or callousness (1 Tim 4:2), and striving to do all for God's glory?

① ② ③ ④ ⑤

Comments

Mission

Worldview

How Christ-centered is your view of reality, holding that in Jesus "the grace of God has appeared, bringing salvation for all people," calling God's people "to live self-controlled, upright, and godly lives in the present age" as they wait "for our blessed hope, the appearing of the glory of our great God and Savior Jesus Christ" (Titus 2:11–13)?

Comments

Commitment

How loyally are you devoting yourself to the things of God to "fight the good fight of the faith" (1 Tim 6:12) and to "wage the good warfare, holding faith and a good conscience" (1 Tim 1:18–19)?

Comments

Environment

How constant are you in enduring hardships, persecutions, trials, and mistreatments, being eager to "share in suffering as a good soldier of Christ Jesus" (2 Tim 2:3)?

Comments

Trust

How confident are you in God's protection over you, believing that "the Lord will rescue [you] from every evil deed and bring [you] safely into his heavenly kingdom" (2 Tim 4:18), having your "hope set on the living God, who is the Savior of all people, especially of those who believe" (1 Tim 4:10)?

Comments

Creation

How attentive are you to steward God's world, neither idolizing nor misusing creation but rather knowing that "everything created by God is good, and nothing is to be rejected if it is received with thanksgiving" (1 Tim 4:4)?

Comments

Community

Relationships

How skillfully are you tending to your relationships by being "above reproach" (1 Tim 3:2) in your personal (3:2–3), family (3:4), church (3:5), world (3:7), and spiritual (3:7) spheres?

① ② ③ ④ ⑤

Comments

Rites/Baptism

How consistent are you being to the faith, striving to "take hold of the eternal life to which you were called and about which you made the good confession in the presence of many witnesses" (1 Tim 6:12)?

① ② ③ ④ ⑤

Comments

Authority

How honorably do you use and respond to God-given authority "so that the name of God and the teaching may not be reviled" (1 Tim 6:1)?

① ② ③ ④ ⑤

Comments

Love

How deeply are you showing a "love that issues from a pure heart and a good conscience and a sincere faith" (1 Tim 1:5)?

① ② ③ ④ ⑤

Comments

Willingness

How available and willing are you to serve God regardless of circumstances, being "a vessel for honorable use, set apart as holy, useful to the master of the house, ready for every good work" (2 Tim 2:21)?

① ② ③ ④ ⑤

Comments

Values

Priorities

How aligned are your values with God's priorities, "storing up treasure for [yourself] as a good foundation for the future, so that [you] may take hold of that which is truly life" (1 Tim 6:19)?

Comments

Truth

How faithful are you in embracing the truth to "agree with the sound words of our Lord Jesus Christ and the teaching that accords with godliness" (1 Tim 6:3), not being "ashamed of the testimony about our Lord" (2 Tim 1:8) nor of the suffering that results from belief in the gospel?

Comments

Passions

How genuinely do you enjoy God's provisions, knowing that "godliness with contentment is great gain" (1 Tim 6:6), not being seduced by "senseless and harmful desires that plunge people into ruin and destruction" (1 Tim 6:9)?

Comments

Sexuality

How pure are you in your sexuality, making sure to abstain from sexual immorality and to "flee youthful passions" (2 Tim 2:22)?

Comments

Conscience

How responsive is your conscience to God and his Word as one of "those who believe and know the truth" (1 Tim 4:3), diligent to "keep a close watch on yourself and on the teaching," remaining vigilant against compromises in life and doctrine (1 Tim 4:16)?

Comments

Habits

Disciplines
How consistently are you practicing the core habits of the faith to "train yourself for godliness" (1 Tim 4:7), believing that "godliness is of value in every way, as it holds promise for the present life and also for the life to come" (1 Tim 4:8)?

① ② ③ ④ ⑤

Comments

Physical Body
How well are you taking care of your physical body, knowing that "bodily training is of some value" for this present life (1 Tim 4:8)?

① ② ③ ④ ⑤

Comments

Speech
How careful are you in your speech, making sure to "in your teaching show integrity, dignity, and sound speech that cannot be condemned, so that an opponent may be put to shame, having nothing evil to say about us" (Tit 2:7–8)?

① ② ③ ④ ⑤

Comments

Time
How wisely do you use your time on a daily basis to strengthen your faith, knowing that "in the last days there will come times of difficulty" (2 Tim 3:1) and that "in later times some will depart from the faith" (1 Tim 4:1)?

① ② ③ ④ ⑤

Comments

Conduct
How discernibly do you live out the ways of God in order to "set the believers an example in speech, in conduct, in love, in faith, in purity" (1 Tim 4:12)?

① ② ③ ④ ⑤

Comments

Celebration

During the past months, what are some key areas to celebrate? What goals were achieved? What progress was made? What lessons were learned? What sense of personal calling and giftedness was confirmed? What unexpected or surprising growth did you experience?

Confession

Over the past quarter, what challenges were encountered? What patterns of sin are being discovered and exposed in your life? What are you learning about yourself that is under the surface of these struggles? What seems to be some of the hang-ups or obstacles to your growth in these areas?

Anticipation

As you anticipate the upcoming months, what are some key goals you want to pursue? What areas of character, knowledge, skill, attitude, or relationship do you want to intentionally pursue? Which goals will you pursue in personal, family, church, and world spheres?

Key Insights

Record noteworthy observations from mentor meetings and peer interaction.

Growth Plan [Q1]

Personal Goals

Identify specific goals from your Progress Report for this upcoming season.

Biblical Rationale

Explain the importance of your goals in light of Scripture.

Action Steps

To achieve your goals, design a plan with concrete, specific, and measurable tasks.

Plan Evaluation

At the end of the season, reflect on your progress in each chosen growth area.

Time Period:

Seasonal Review
Quarter 2

The following pages outline a pathway for your **second** seasonal review of the year. This series of exercises is meant to give you some space to appraise your progress over the past quarter as well as envision a plan for the upcoming months. Take time for this life audit by completing the personal inventory, summarizing a progress report, seeking mentor feedback, and composing a growth plan. Try to make this both a personal time as well as a time where key mentors and those in your church community are invited into the reflection and planning process.

Identity

Conversion

How apparent is your conversion to the faith as one who has come to "believe in [Jesus] for eternal life" (1 Tim 1:16), being able to confess "that Christ Jesus came into the world to save sinners, of whom I am the foremost" (1 Tim 1:15)?

① ② ③ ④ ⑤

Comments

Character

How evidently are you embodying a holy life that is "above reproach" (1 Tim 3:2) by fleeing all godlessness to "pursue righteousness, godliness, faith, love, steadfastness, gentleness" (1 Tim 6:11)?

① ② ③ ④ ⑤

Comments

Progress

How dutifully are you giving yourself to your own faith formation in practice, devotion, and persistence "so that all may see your progress" (1 Tim 4:15)?

① ② ③ ④ ⑤

Comments

Approval

How concerned are you ultimately about God's opinion of you in all things (not the opinions of men) that you "do your best to present yourself to God as one approved" (2 Tim 2:15)?

① ② ③ ④ ⑤

Comments

Emotions

How maturely do you live out of healthy emotions, taking confidence that "God gave us a spirit not of fear but of power and love and self-control" (2 Tim 1:7)?

① ② ③ ④ ⑤

Comments

Vocation

Self-Awareness/Giftedness
How aware are you of God's calling on your life to "fulfill your ministry" (2 Tim 4:5), being careful to not "neglect the gift you have" (1 Tim 4:14) but rather "to fan into flame the gift of God" (2 Tim 1:6) which has been given to you?

① ② ③ ④ ⑤

Comments

Skills
How competent are you becoming in your life and ministry skills, doing "your best to present yourself to God as one approved, a worker who has no need to be ashamed, rightly handling the word of truth" (2 Tim 2:15)?

① ② ③ ④ ⑤

Comments

Resources
How responsibly are you using your resources toward an eternal investment to "be rich in good works" and "generous and ready to share," not setting "hopes on the uncertainty of riches, but on God, who richly provides us with everything to enjoy" (1 Tim 6:17–18)?

① ② ③ ④ ⑤

Comments

Work
How conscientious are you in your vocation, performing it as a ministry toward God as would a hard-working farmer, fully devoted athlete, and duty-bound soldier (2 Tim 2:3–7)?

① ② ③ ④ ⑤

Comments

Motivations
How sincerely are your motivations coming from a "pure heart" (1 Tim 1:5), receiving God's good gifts "with thanksgiving," (1 Tim 4:4) not being given to insincerity, deception, or callousness (1 Tim 4:2), and striving to do all for God's glory?

① ② ③ ④ ⑤

Comments

Mission

Worldview

How Christ-centered is your view of reality, holding that in Jesus "the grace of God has appeared, bringing salvation for all people," calling God's people "to live self-controlled, upright, and godly lives in the present age" as they wait "for our blessed hope, the appearing of the glory of our great God and Savior Jesus Christ" (Titus 2:11–13)?

Comments

Commitment

How loyally are you devoting yourself to the things of God to "fight the good fight of the faith" (1 Tim 6:12) and to "wage the good warfare, holding faith and a good conscience" (1 Tim 1:18–19)?

Comments

Environment

How constant are you in enduring hardships, persecutions, trials, and mistreatments, being eager to "share in suffering as a good soldier of Christ Jesus" (2 Tim 2:3)?

Comments

Trust

How confident are you in God's protection over you, believing that "the Lord will rescue [you] from every evil deed and bring [you] safely into his heavenly kingdom" (2 Tim 4:18), having your "hope set on the living God, who is the Savior of all people, especially of those who believe" (1 Tim 4:10)?

Comments

Creation

How attentive are you to steward God's world, neither idolizing nor misusing creation but rather knowing that "everything created by God is good, and nothing is to be rejected if it is received with thanksgiving" (1 Tim 4:4)?

Comments

Community

Relationships
How skillfully are you tending to your relationships by being "above reproach" (1 Tim 3:2) in your personal (3:2–3), family (3:4), church (3:5), world (3:7), and spiritual (3:7) spheres?

① ② ③ ④ ⑤

Comments

Rites/Baptism
How consistent are you being to the faith, striving to "take hold of the eternal life to which you were called and about which you made the good confession in the presence of many witnesses" (1 Tim 6:12)?

① ② ③ ④ ⑤

Comments

Authority
How honorably do you use and respond to God-given authority "so that the name of God and the teaching may not be reviled" (1 Tim 6:1)?

① ② ③ ④ ⑤

Comments

Love
How deeply are you showing a "love that issues from a pure heart and a good conscience and a sincere faith" (1 Tim 1:5)?

① ② ③ ④ ⑤

Comments

Willingness
How available and willing are you to serve God regardless of circumstances, being "a vessel for honorable use, set apart as holy, useful to the master of the house, ready for every good work" (2 Tim 2:21)?

① ② ③ ④ ⑤

Comments

Values

Priorities

How aligned are your values with God's priorities, "storing up treasure for [yourself] as a good foundation for the future, so that [you] may take hold of that which is truly life" (1 Tim 6:19)?

Comments

Truth

How faithful are you in embracing the truth to "agree with the sound words of our Lord Jesus Christ and the teaching that accords with godliness" (1 Tim 6:3), not being "ashamed of the testimony about our Lord" (2 Tim 1:8) nor of the suffering that results from belief in the gospel?

Comments

Passions

How genuinely do you enjoy God's provisions, knowing that "godliness with contentment is great gain" (1 Tim 6:6), not being seduced by "senseless and harmful desires that plunge people into ruin and destruction" (1 Tim 6:9)?

Comments

Sexuality

How pure are you in your sexuality, making sure to abstain from sexual immorality and to "flee youthful passions" (2 Tim 2:22)?

Comments

Conscience

How responsive is your conscience to God and his Word as one of "those who believe and know the truth" (1 Tim 4:3), diligent to "keep a close watch on yourself and on the teaching," remaining vigilant against compromises in life and doctrine (1 Tim 4:16)?

Comments

Habits

Disciplines
How consistently are you practicing the core habits of the faith to "train yourself for godliness" (1 Tim 4:7), believing that "godliness is of value in every way, as it holds promise for the present life and also for the life to come" (1 Tim 4:8)?

① ② ③ ④ ⑤

Comments

Physical Body
How well are you taking care of your physical body, knowing that "bodily training is of some value" for this present life (1 Tim 4:8)?

① ② ③ ④ ⑤

Comments

Speech
How careful are you in your speech, making sure to "in your teaching show integrity, dignity, and sound speech that cannot be condemned, so that an opponent may be put to shame, having nothing evil to say about us" (Tit 2:7–8)?

① ② ③ ④ ⑤

Comments

Time
How wisely do you use your time on a daily basis to strengthen your faith, knowing that "in the last days there will come times of difficulty" (2 Tim 3:1) and that "in later times some will depart from the faith" (1 Tim 4:1)?

① ② ③ ④ ⑤

Comments

Conduct
How discernibly do you live out the ways of God in order to "set the believers an example in speech, in conduct, in love, in faith, in purity" (1 Tim 4:12)?

① ② ③ ④ ⑤

Comments

Celebration

During the past months, what are some key areas to celebrate? What goals were achieved? What progress was made? What lessons were learned? What sense of personal calling and giftedness was confirmed? What unexpected or surprising growth did you experience?

Confession

Over the past quarter, what challenges were encountered? What patterns of sin are being discovered and exposed in your life? What are you learning about yourself that is under the surface of these struggles? What seems to be some of the hang-ups or obstacles to your growth in these areas?

Anticipation

As you anticipate the upcoming months, what are some key goals you want to pursue? What areas of character, knowledge, skill, attitude, or relationship do you want to intentionally pursue? Which goals will you pursue in personal, family, church, and world spheres?

Community Feedback [Q2]

Key Insights

Record noteworthy observations from mentor meetings and peer interaction.

Growth Plan [Q2]

Personal Goals

Identify specific goals from your Progress Report for this upcoming season.

Biblical Rationale

Explain the importance of your goals in light of Scripture.

Action Steps

To achieve your goals, design a plan with concrete, specific, and measurable tasks.

Plan Evaluation

At the end of the season, reflect on your progress in each chosen growth area.

Time Period:

Seasonal Review
Quarter 3

The following pages outline a pathway for your **third** seasonal review of the year. This series of exercises is meant to give you some space to appraise your progress over the past quarter as well as envision a plan for the upcoming months. Take time for this life audit by completing the personal inventory, summarizing a progress report, seeking mentor feedback, and composing a growth plan. Try to make this both a personal time as well as a time where key mentors and those in your church community are invited into the reflection and planning process.

Identity

Conversion

How apparent is your conversion to the faith as one who has come to "believe in [Jesus] for eternal life" (1 Tim 1:16), being able to confess "that Christ Jesus came into the world to save sinners, of whom I am the foremost" (1 Tim 1:15)?

Comments

Character

How evidently are you embodying a holy life that is "above reproach" (1 Tim 3:2) by fleeing all godlessness to "pursue righteousness, godliness, faith, love, steadfastness, gentleness" (1 Tim 6:11)?

Comments

Progress

How dutifully are you giving yourself to your own faith formation in practice, devotion, and persistence "so that all may see your progress" (1 Tim 4:15)?

Comments

Approval

How concerned are you ultimately about God's opinion of you in all things (not the opinions of men) that you "do your best to present yourself to God as one approved" (2 Tim 2:15)?

Comments

Emotions

How maturely do you live out of healthy emotions, taking confidence that "God gave us a spirit not of fear but of power and love and self-control" (2 Tim 1:7)?

Comments

Vocation

Self-Awareness/Giftedness

How aware are you of God's calling on your life to "fulfill your ministry" (2 Tim 4:5), being careful to not "neglect the gift you have" (1 Tim 4:14) but rather "to fan into flame the gift of God" (2 Tim 1:6) which has been given to you?

① ② ③ ④ ⑤

Comments

Skills

How competent are you becoming in your life and ministry skills, doing "your best to present yourself to God as one approved, a worker who has no need to be ashamed, rightly handling the word of truth" (2 Tim 2:15)?

① ② ③ ④ ⑤

Comments

Resources

How responsibly are you using your resources toward an eternal investment to "be rich in good works" and "generous and ready to share," not setting "hopes on the uncertainty of riches, but on God, who richly provides us with everything to enjoy" (1 Tim 6:17–18)?

① ② ③ ④ ⑤

Comments

Work

How conscientious are you in your vocation, performing it as a ministry toward God as would a hard-working farmer, fully devoted athlete, and duty-bound soldier (2 Tim 2:3–7)?

① ② ③ ④ ⑤

Comments

Motivations

How sincerely are your motivations coming from a "pure heart" (1 Tim 1:5), receiving God's good gifts "with thanksgiving," (1 Tim 4:4) not being given to insincerity, deception, or callousness (1 Tim 4:2), and striving to do all for God's glory?

① ② ③ ④ ⑤

Comments

Mission

Worldview

How Christ-centered is your view of reality, holding that in Jesus "the grace of God has appeared, bringing salvation for all people," calling God's people "to live self-controlled, upright, and godly lives in the present age" as they wait "for our blessed hope, the appearing of the glory of our great God and Savior Jesus Christ" (Titus 2:11–13)?

Comments

Commitment

How loyally are you devoting yourself to the things of God to "fight the good fight of the faith" (1 Tim 6:12) and to "wage the good warfare, holding faith and a good conscience" (1 Tim 1:18–19)?

Comments

Environment

How constant are you in enduring hardships, persecutions, trials, and mistreatments, being eager to "share in suffering as a good soldier of Christ Jesus" (2 Tim 2:3)?

Comments

Trust

How confident are you in God's protection over you, believing that "the Lord will rescue [you] from every evil deed and bring [you] safely into his heavenly kingdom" (2 Tim 4:18), having your "hope set on the living God, who is the Savior of all people, especially of those who believe" (1 Tim 4:10)?

Comments

Creation

How attentive are you to steward God's world, neither idolizing nor misusing creation but rather knowing that "everything created by God is good, and nothing is to be rejected if it is received with thanksgiving" (1 Tim 4:4)?

Comments

Community

Relationships
How skillfully are you tending to your relationships by being "above reproach" (1 Tim 3:2) in your personal (3:2–3), family (3:4), church (3:5), world (3:7), and spiritual (3:7) spheres?

① ② ③ ④ ⑤

Comments

Rites/Baptism
How consistent are you being to the faith, striving to "take hold of the eternal life to which you were called and about which you made the good confession in the presence of many witnesses" (1 Tim 6:12)?

① ② ③ ④ ⑤

Comments

Authority
How honorably do you use and respond to God-given authority "so that the name of God and the teaching may not be reviled" (1 Tim 6:1)?

① ② ③ ④ ⑤

Comments

Love
How deeply are you showing a "love that issues from a pure heart and a good conscience and a sincere faith" (1 Tim 1:5)?

① ② ③ ④ ⑤

Comments

Willingness
How available and willing are you to serve God regardless of circumstances, being "a vessel for honorable use, set apart as holy, useful to the master of the house, ready for every good work" (2 Tim 2:21)?

① ② ③ ④ ⑤

Comments

Values

Priorities

How aligned are your values with God's priorities, "storing up treasure for [yourself] as a good foundation for the future, so that [you] may take hold of that which is truly life" (1 Tim 6:19)?

Comments

Truth

How faithful are you in embracing the truth to "agree with the sound words of our Lord Jesus Christ and the teaching that accords with godliness" (1 Tim 6:3), not being "ashamed of the testimony about our Lord" (2 Tim 1:8) nor of the suffering that results from belief in the gospel?

Comments

Passions

How genuinely do you enjoy God's provisions, knowing that "godliness with contentment is great gain" (1 Tim 6:6), not being seduced by "senseless and harmful desires that plunge people into ruin and destruction" (1 Tim 6:9)?

Comments

Sexuality

How pure are you in your sexuality, making sure to abstain from sexual immorality and to "flee youthful passions" (2 Tim 2:22)?

Comments

Conscience

How responsive is your conscience to God and his Word as one of "those who believe and know the truth" (1 Tim 4:3), diligent to "keep a close watch on yourself and on the teaching," remaining vigilant against compromises in life and doctrine (1 Tim 4:16)?

Comments

Habits

Disciplines
How consistently are you practicing the core habits of the faith to "train yourself for godliness" (1 Tim 4:7), believing that "godliness is of value in every way, as it holds promise for the present life and also for the life to come" (1 Tim 4:8)?

① ② ③ ④ ⑤

Comments

Physical Body
How well are you taking care of your physical body, knowing that "bodily training is of some value" for this present life (1 Tim 4:8)?

① ② ③ ④ ⑤

Comments

Speech
How careful are you in your speech, making sure to "in your teaching show integrity, dignity, and sound speech that cannot be condemned, so that an opponent may be put to shame, having nothing evil to say about us" (Tit 2:7–8)?

① ② ③ ④ ⑤

Comments

Time
How wisely do you use your time on a daily basis to strengthen your faith, knowing that "in the last days there will come times of difficulty" (2 Tim 3:1) and that "in later times some will depart from the faith" (1 Tim 4:1)?

① ② ③ ④ ⑤

Comments

Conduct
How discernibly do you live out the ways of God in order to "set the believers an example in speech, in conduct, in love, in faith, in purity" (1 Tim 4:12)?

① ② ③ ④ ⑤

Comments

Celebration

During the past months, what are some key areas to celebrate? What goals were achieved? What progress was made? What lessons were learned? What sense of personal calling and giftedness was confirmed? What unexpected or surprising growth did you experience?

Confession

Over the past quarter, what challenges were encountered? What patterns of sin are being discovered and exposed in your life? What are you learning about yourself that is under the surface of these struggles? What seems to be some of the hang-ups or obstacles to your growth in these areas?

Anticipation

As you anticipate the upcoming months, what are some key goals you want to pursue? What areas of character, knowledge, skill, attitude, or relationship do you want to intentionally pursue? Which goals will you pursue in personal, family, church, and world spheres?

Key Insights

Record noteworthy observations from mentor meetings and peer interaction.

Personal Goals

Identify specific goals from your Progress Report for this upcoming season.

Biblical Rationale

Explain the importance of your goals in light of Scripture.

Action Steps

To achieve your goals, design a plan with concrete, specific, and measurable tasks.

Plan Evaluation

At the end of the season, reflect on your progress in each chosen growth area.

Time Period:

Seasonal Review
Quarter 4

The following pages outline a pathway for your **fourth** seasonal review of the year. This series of exercises is meant to give you some space to appraise your progress over the past quarter as well as envision a plan for the upcoming months. Take time for this life audit by completing the personal inventory, summarizing a progress report, seeking mentor feedback, and composing a growth plan. Try to make this both a personal time as well as a time where key mentors and those in your church community are invited into the reflection and planning process.

Identity

Conversion

How apparent is your conversion to the faith as one who has come to "believe in [Jesus] for eternal life" (1 Tim 1:16), being able to confess "that Christ Jesus came into the world to save sinners, of whom I am the foremost" (1 Tim 1:15)?

Comments

Character

How evidently are you embodying a holy life that is "above reproach" (1 Tim 3:2) by fleeing all godlessness to "pursue righteousness, godliness, faith, love, steadfastness, gentleness" (1 Tim 6:11)?

Comments

Progress

How dutifully are you giving yourself to your own faith formation in practice, devotion, and persistence "so that all may see your progress" (1 Tim 4:15)?

Comments

Approval

How concerned are you ultimately about God's opinion of you in all things (not the opinions of men) that you "do your best to present yourself to God as one approved" (2 Tim 2:15)?

Comments

Emotions

How maturely do you live out of healthy emotions, taking confidence that "God gave us a spirit not of fear but of power and love and self-control" (2 Tim 1:7)?

Comments

Vocation

Self-Awareness/Giftedness

How aware are you of God's calling on your life to "fulfill your ministry" (2 Tim 4:5), being careful to not "neglect the gift you have" (1 Tim 4:14) but rather "to fan into flame the gift of God" (2 Tim 1:6) which has been given to you?

① ② ③ ④ ⑤

Comments

Skills

How competent are you becoming in your life and ministry skills, doing "your best to present yourself to God as one approved, a worker who has no need to be ashamed, rightly handling the word of truth" (2 Tim 2:15)?

① ② ③ ④ ⑤

Comments

Resources

How responsibly are you using your resources toward an eternal investment to "be rich in good works" and "generous and ready to share," not setting "hopes on the uncertainty of riches, but on God, who richly provides us with everything to enjoy" (1 Tim 6:17–18)?

① ② ③ ④ ⑤

Comments

Work

How conscientious are you in your vocation, performing it as a ministry toward God as would a hard-working farmer, fully devoted athlete, and duty-bound soldier (2 Tim 2:3–7)?

① ② ③ ④ ⑤

Comments

Motivations

How sincerely are your motivations coming from a "pure heart" (1 Tim 1:5), receiving God's good gifts "with thanksgiving," (1 Tim 4:4) not being given to insincerity, deception, or callousness (1 Tim 4:2), and striving to do all for God's glory?

① ② ③ ④ ⑤

Comments

Mission

Worldview

How Christ-centered is your view of reality, holding that in Jesus "the grace of God has appeared, bringing salvation for all people," calling God's people "to live self-controlled, upright, and godly lives in the present age" as they wait "for our blessed hope, the appearing of the glory of our great God and Savior Jesus Christ" (Titus 2:11–13)?

① ② ③ ④ ⑤

Comments

Commitment

How loyally are you devoting yourself to the things of God to "fight the good fight of the faith" (1 Tim 6:12) and to "wage the good warfare, holding faith and a good conscience" (1 Tim 1:18–19)?

① ② ③ ④ ⑤

Comments

Environment

How constant are you in enduring hardships, persecutions, trials, and mistreatments, being eager to "share in suffering as a good soldier of Christ Jesus" (2 Tim 2:3)?

① ② ③ ④ ⑤

Comments

Trust

How confident are you in God's protection over you, believing that "the Lord will rescue [you] from every evil deed and bring [you] safely into his heavenly kingdom" (2 Tim 4:18), having your "hope set on the living God, who is the Savior of all people, especially of those who believe" (1 Tim 4:10)?

① ② ③ ④ ⑤

Comments

Creation

How attentive are you to steward God's world, neither idolizing nor misusing creation but rather knowing that "everything created by God is good, and nothing is to be rejected if it is received with thanksgiving" (1 Tim 4:4)?

① ② ③ ④ ⑤

Comments

Community

Relationships
How skillfully are you tending to your relationships by being "above reproach" (1 Tim 3:2) in your personal (3:2–3), family (3:4), church (3:5), world (3:7), and spiritual (3:7) spheres?

① ② ③ ④ ⑤

Comments

Rites/Baptism
How consistent are you being to the faith, striving to "take hold of the eternal life to which you were called and about which you made the good confession in the presence of many witnesses" (1 Tim 6:12)?

① ② ③ ④ ⑤

Comments

Authority
How honorably do you use and respond to God-given authority "so that the name of God and the teaching may not be reviled" (1 Tim 6:1)?

① ② ③ ④ ⑤

Comments

Love
How deeply are you showing a "love that issues from a pure heart and a good conscience and a sincere faith" (1 Tim 1:5)?

① ② ③ ④ ⑤

Comments

Willingness
How available and willing are you to serve God regardless of circumstances, being "a vessel for honorable use, set apart as holy, useful to the master of the house, ready for every good work" (2 Tim 2:21)?

① ② ③ ④ ⑤

Comments

Values

Priorities

How aligned are your values with God's priorities, "storing up treasure for [yourself] as a good foundation for the future, so that [you] may take hold of that which is truly life" (1 Tim 6:19)?

Comments

Truth

How faithful are you in embracing the truth to "agree with the sound words of our Lord Jesus Christ and the teaching that accords with godliness" (1 Tim 6:3), not being "ashamed of the testimony about our Lord" (2 Tim 1:8) nor of the suffering that results from belief in the gospel?

Comments

Passions

How genuinely do you enjoy God's provisions, knowing that "godliness with contentment is great gain" (1 Tim 6:6), not being seduced by "senseless and harmful desires that plunge people into ruin and destruction" (1 Tim 6:9)?

Comments

Sexuality

How pure are you in your sexuality, making sure to abstain from sexual immorality and to "flee youthful passions" (2 Tim 2:22)?

Comments

Conscience

How responsive is your conscience to God and his Word as one of "those who believe and know the truth" (1 Tim 4:3), diligent to "keep a close watch on yourself and on the teaching," remaining vigilant against compromises in life and doctrine (1 Tim 4:16)?

Comments

Habits

Disciplines
How consistently are you practicing the core habits of the faith to "train yourself for godliness" (1 Tim 4:7), believing that "godliness is of value in every way, as it holds promise for the present life and also for the life to come" (1 Tim 4:8)?

① ② ③ ④ ⑤

Comments

Physical Body
How well are you taking care of your physical body, knowing that "bodily training is of some value" for this present life (1 Tim 4:8)?

① ② ③ ④ ⑤

Comments

Speech
How careful are you in your speech, making sure to "in your teaching show integrity, dignity, and sound speech that cannot be condemned, so that an opponent may be put to shame, having nothing evil to say about us" (Tit 2:7–8)?

① ② ③ ④ ⑤

Comments

Time
How wisely do you use your time on a daily basis to strengthen your faith, knowing that "in the last days there will come times of difficulty" (2 Tim 3:1) and that "in later times some will depart from the faith" (1 Tim 4:1)?

① ② ③ ④ ⑤

Comments

Conduct
How discernibly do you live out the ways of God in order to "set the believers an example in speech, in conduct, in love, in faith, in purity" (1 Tim 4:12)?

① ② ③ ④ ⑤

Comments

Celebration

During the past months, what are some key areas to celebrate? What goals were achieved? What progress was made? What lessons were learned? What sense of personal calling and giftedness was confirmed? What unexpected or surprising growth did you experience?

Confession

Over the past quarter, what challenges were encountered? What patterns of sin are being discovered and exposed in your life? What are you learning about yourself that is under the surface of these struggles? What seems to be some of the hang-ups or obstacles to your growth in these areas?

Anticipation

As you anticipate the upcoming months, what are some key goals you want to pursue? What areas of character, knowledge, skill, attitude, or relationship do you want to intentionally pursue? Which goals will you pursue in personal, family, church, and world spheres?

Community Feedback [Q4]

Key Insights

Record noteworthy observations from mentor meetings and peer interaction.

Personal Goals

Identify specific goals from your Progress Report for this upcoming season.

Biblical Rationale

Explain the importance of your goals in light of Scripture.

Action Steps

To achieve your goals, design a plan with concrete, specific, and measurable tasks.

Plan Evaluation

At the end of the season, reflect on your progress in each chosen growth area.

Personal Memoirs

Sensing God's Movement in the Daily Journey

....

The third movement of this journal, **Personal Memoirs**, is open journal space. This portion of the journal is intended as processing space for you to log spiritual insights, record daily spiritual practices, track weekly progress, and use for any other markings that you consider important along your journey.

207

217

Further Resources

Charting the Course for Ongoing Formation

The final part of this journal is for your further development. The following pages of this **Further Resources** section provide resources that can aid you in your lifelong process of spiritual formation.

Morning Communion
Spiritual Reading

Lectio Divina

Spiritual Reading (*lectio divina*) fosters prayerful and reflective reading of the Scriptures. By immersing yourself in a portion of Scripture, you allow the Scripture itself to guide your prayer back to God. As you work through a passage of Scripture, take time to read a section of the passage, reflect on its meaning, and then respond with the text in prayer.

"He who wishes to always be with God must often pray and often read. For when we pray, we speak with God; when we read God speaks to us." [30]

Isidore of Seville, *Sentences*

....

"Your word is a lamp to my feet and a light to my path."

Psalm 119:105

Select a Scripture

Identify a passage of the Bible, choosing a portion that is manageable in size.

Here are a few examples of prayerful texts:
1 Samuel 2:1–10; 1 Kings 8:54–61; Nehemiah 1:4–11; Psalm 90:1–17; Isaiah 37:14–20; Daniel 9:3–19; Mark 14:32–42; Acts 4:23–31; 20:17–38; Romans 1:8–17; Ephesians 1:15–23; 3:14–21; Colossians 1:3–8; 4:2–6; Philemon 4–7; Revelation 4:1–5:14.

Read the Passage (*lectio*)

Engage the passage of Scripture, paying attention to its movement and flow.

Reflect on its Meaning (*meditatio*)

Contemplate the passage, taking notice of important observations or insights.

Respond with the Text (*oratio*)

Pray the passage back to God, allowing the details of the text to inform your petition.

Evening Review
Self-Examination

Daily examen is a practice of communing with the Lord, reflecting on the past day, and anticipating the day to follow. It seeks to build a habit and rhythm of life in which we acknowledge God's presence, take time for gratitude, confess our failures, and recommit ourselves to God's ways for the next day ahead.

"Make up your spiritual accounts daily; see how matters stand between God and your souls…Often reckonings keep God and conscience friends. Do with your hearts as you do with your watches, wind them up every morning by prayer, and at night examine whether your hearts have gone true all that day." [31]

Thomas Watson, *A Body of Practical Divinity*

"Search me, O God, and know my heart! Try me and know my thoughts! And see if there be any grievous way in me, and lead me in the way everlasting!"

Psalm 139:23–24

Acknowledge God's Presence

Meditate — Take a moment to pause, be silent, and acknowledge God's presence.

"Where shall I go from your Spirit? Or where shall I flee from your presence?" *(Psalm 139:7)*

Pray — As you rest before God, offer this plea for God's mercy.

"God, be merciful to me, a sinner!" *(Luke 18:13)*

Reflect in Gratitude

Reflect — Contemplate the events of your day, your interactions with people, and the emotions during those times.

Record — In gratitude, note the times you have seen God's presence or hand at work. Where did God show up in your life today?

Remember with Honesty

Reflect — Consider the opportunities where you missed the Lord's presence or did not take His invitation to grace.

Record — In humility, note the times you have missed God's leading or failed to notice His hand at work. What were the missed opportunities of the past day?

Make Future Commitments

Reflect — Take time to consider what it would look like to be more aware and open to God's presence in the upcoming day. What kind of future commitments will you make moving forward?

Pray — "It is the Lord who goes before you. He will be with you; he will not leave you or forsake you. Do not fear or be dismayed." *(Deuteronomy 31:8)*

Weekly Review
Personal Reflection

At the end of the week, take time to use the following questions to reflect on your past week. Take space to quiet your mind and heart and assess key events, meaningful opportunities, and vital lessons that occurred. Use journal space to reflect in word, diagram, drawing, or other creative expressions of what you think God is doing in your own heart. Specifically, celebrate God's movement in the six undercurrents of your life: identity, vocation, mission, community, values, and habits.

"And only when they made a holy day for God did they find they had made a holiday for men." [32]

Gilbert K. Chesterton, *Orthodoxy*

"Let the words of my mouth and the meditation of my heart be acceptable in your sight, O Lord, my rock and my redeemer."

Psalm 19:14

Gazing Inward at God's Design

Identity — In this past week, how did you deepen your understanding of God? How did you grow in your understanding of yourself?

Vocation — How did you exercise your gifts this past week in the service of others? How did you grow in your understanding of your unique God-given design?

Looking Outward at God's Work

Mission — What opportunities did God give you to live on mission this week? How well do you feel you took advantage of these opportunities?

Community — What kind of meaningful investments and connections did you make with relationships this week in family, church, and world spheres?

Reflecting Upward at God's Ways

Values — How well did you keep your focus on God's priorities in your various spheres of life? Can you identify any misplaced priorities in your life at this time?

Habits — How would you evaluate your habits and life rhythms over this past week? What are some of the things you think God is calling you to work on during the next week?

Monthly Meal

Dinner Conversation

Table Talk

Enjoy a monthly meal with a trusted mentor in your church community. Take time to relish the table fellowship, edifying conversation, and mutual encouragement that Christian community uniquely affords. Use the following questions as conversation starters to facilitate meaningful dialogue around the meal.

> "Come ye hither all, whose taste
>   Is our waste;
> Save your cost, and mend your fare.
> God is here prepared and dressed,
> And the feast,
>   God, in whom all dainties are." [33]
>
> George Herbert, "The Invitation"

....

> "And day by day, attending the temple together and breaking bread in their homes, they received their food with glad and generous hearts, praising God and having favor with all the people."
>
> Acts 2:46–47

Recalling God's Movements

How have you noticed God at work in your midst?
How has God shown himself faithful, sovereign, loving, patient, just, and merciful?
What stories can you tell to express gratitude for God's continued work and active presence in your life?

Naming Personal Struggles

What challenges have you encountered during the past weeks?
How might these difficulties be an opportunity to grow and mature in your faith?
What are these challenges teaching you about yourself and God?

Seeking Community Support

How would you want to see yourself grow in the upcoming weeks?
What specific resources or help do you need in order to experience this growth?
How can you specifically pray for each other?

Hearing Spiritual Feedback

What are specific areas in your life that need to be addressed?
How have you grown in ways that are worth celebrating?

Essentials Library

Discipleship and the Christian Life

à Kempis, Thomas. *Of the Imitation of Christ*. Oxford: Rivingtons, 1876.

Bonhoeffer, Dietrich. *The Cost of Discipleship*. New York: Touchstone, 2018.

Law, William. *A Serious Call to a Devout and Holy Life*. Mineola: Dover Publications, 2013.

Perkins, William. *A Treatise of the Vocations*. Cambridge: John Legat, 1605.

Schaeffer, Francis A. *True Spirituality*. In The Complete Works of Francis A. Schaeffer: A Christian Worldview, vol. 3. Westchester: Crossway Books, 1982.

Taylor, Jeremy. *Holy Living and Dying*. New York: D. Appleton, 1865.

Spiritual Formation

Bennett, Arthur. *The Valley of Vision: A Collection of Puritan Prayers and Devotions*. Edinburgh: Banner of Truth Trust, 1975.

Brother Lawrence. *The Practice of the Presence of God*. Heart and Life Booklets 11. London: H. R. Allenson, 1906.

Bunyan, John. *The Pilgrim's Progress*. New York: P. F. Collier & Son, 1909.

Burroughs, Jeremiah. *The Rare Jewel of Christian Contentment*. London: John Streater, 1670.

Herbert, George. *Herbert's Poems*. New York: E. & J. B. Young and Company, 1903.

Murray, Andrew. *Humility: The Beauty of Holiness*. London: James Nisbet & Company, 1896.

Pascal, Blaise. *Thoughts, Letters, and Minor Works*. Edited by Charles W. Eliot. Translated by W. F. Trotter, M. L. Booth, and O. W. Wight, The Harvard Classics 48. New York: P. F. Collier & Son, 1910.

Saint John of the Cross. *The Dark Night of the Soul*. Translated by Gabriela Cunninghame Graham. London: John M. Watkins, 1905.

Basic Christian Theology

Athanasius. *On the Incarnation*. Translated by John Behr. Yonkers: St. Vladimir's Seminary Press, 2011.

Augustine. *The Confessions*. Translated by Maria Boulding. Vintage Spiritual Classics. New York: Vintage Books, 1998.

Calvin, John. *Institutes of the Christian Religion*. Translated by Henry Beveridge. Peabody: Hendrickson Publishers, 2008.

Chesterton, Gilbert K. *Orthodoxy*. New York: John Lane Company, 1909.

Lewis, C. S. *Mere Christianity*. New York: HarperOne, 2001.

Packer, J. I. *Knowing God*. Downers Grove: InterVarsity, 1993.

Stott, John. *Basic Christianity*. Downers Grove: InterVarsity, 2021.

Watson, Thomas. *A Body of Practical Divinity*. London: Thomas Parkhurst, 1692.

Community Life

Bonhoeffer, Dietrich. *Life Together*. New York: Harper & Row Publishers, 1954.

Bonhoeffer, Dietrich. *The Communion of Saints: A Dogmatic Inquiry into the Sociology of the Church*. Translated by R. Gregor Smith. New York: Harper & Row, Publishers, 1963.

Newbigin, Lesslie. *The Household of God: Lectures on the Nature of the Church*. Eugene: Wipf and Stock, 2008.

Schaeffer, Francis A. *The Church Before the Watching World*. In The Complete Works of Francis A. Schaeffer: A Christian Worldview, vol. 3. Westchester: Crossway Books, 1982.

Ministry and Mission

Allen, Roland. *Missionary Methods: St. Paul's or Ours?* London: Robert Scott, 1912.

Baxter, Richard. *The Reformed Pastor*. Edinburgh: The Banner of Truth Trust, 2001.

Chrysostom, John. *Six Books on the Priesthood*. Popular Patristics Series 1. St. Vladimir's Seminary Press, 1964.

Gregory the Great. *The Book of Pastoral Rule*. Translated by George E. Demacopoulos. Popular Patristics Series 34. Edited by John Behr. Crestwood: St. Vladimir's Seminary Press, 2007.

Spurgeon, Charles H. *Lectures to My Students*. New York: Sheldon & Company, 1875.

Classic Fiction

Bernanos, George. *The Diary of a Country Priest*. New York: Carroll & Graf Publishers, 2002.

Dickens, Charles. *Great Expectations*. The Works of Charles Dickens 13. London: Chapman & Hall, 1901.

Dostoyevsky, Fyodor. *The Brothers Karamazov*. Translated by Constance Garnett. New York: Macmillan, 1922.

Hawthorne, Nathaniel. *The Scarlet Letter, a Romance*. Boston: Ticknor, Reed and Fields, 1850.

End Notes

1. Charles Spurgeon, "Obadiah; Or, Early Piety Eminent Piety," in *The Metropolitan Tabernacle Pulpit Sermons* 30 (London: Passmore & Alabaster, 1884), 558.

2. Thomas Aquinas, *The "Summa Theologica" of St. Thomas Aquinas*, trans. Fathers of the English Dominican Province, Part 2 (First Part), volume 6 (London: R & T Washbourne, 1914), 376.

3. Blaise Pascal, *Thoughts, Letters, and Minor Works*, ed. Charles W. Eliot, trans. W. F. Trotter, M. L. Booth, and O. W. Wight, The Harvard Classics 48 (New York: P. F. Collier & Son, 1910), 40.

4. Dietrich Bonhoeffer, *The Communion of Saints: A Dogmatic Inquiry into the Sociology of the Church*, translated by R. Gregor Smith (New York: Harper & Row, Publishers, 1963), 48. From The Communion of Saints by Dietrich Bonhoeffer. Copyright © 1960 by Christian Kaiser Verlag. Copyright © 1963 in the English translation by William Collins Sons & Co.Ltd., London, and Harper & Row, Inc., New York. Copyright renewed 1991. Used by permission of HarperCollins Publishers.

5. C. S. Lewis, *Mere Christianity* (New York: HarperOne, 2001), 225-227. MERE CHRISTIANITY by CS Lewis © copyright CS Lewis Pte Ltd 1942, 1943, 1944, 1952. Used by permission.

6. Adapted from John Calvin, *Institutes of the Christian Religion*, vol. 2 (Edinburgh: The Calvin Translation Society, 1845), 47-48.

7. Adapted from Janet O. Hagberg and Robert A. Guelich, *The Critical Journey: Stages in the Life of Faith* (Salem: Sheffield Publishing Company, 2005). Reprinted by permission of Sheffield Publishing Co. from Hagberg-Guelich, THE CRITICAL JOURNEY, SECOND EDITION, Salem, WI: Sheffield Publishing Company, copyright 2005. All rights reserved.

8. William Perkins, *A Treatise of the Vocations* (Cambridge: John Legat, 1605), 909.

9. Dorothy L. Sayers, "Why Work?," in *Letters to a Diminished Church: Passionate Arguments for the Relevance of Christian Doctrine* (Nashville: W Publishing Group, 2004) 118-139. Taken from *Letters to a Diminished Church* by Dorothy L. Sayers. Copyright © 2004 by W. Publishing Group, a division of Thomas Nelson, Inc. Used by permission of Thomas Nelson. www.thomasnelson.com.

10. Karl Barth, "Vocation," in *Church Dogmatics: The Doctrine of Creation*, Geoffrey William Bromiley, and Thomas F. Torrance, eds., Part 4, vol. 3 (Edinburgh: T&T Clark, 2004), 624. Copyright © Karl Barth, 2004, Church Dogmatics: The Doctrine of Creation, T&T Clark, an imprint of Bloomsbury Publishing Plc. Used by permission.

11. Arthur F. Miller, *The Power of Uniqueness: How to Become Who You Really Are* (Grand Rapids: Zondervan, 2002). Taken from *The Power of Uniqueness: How to Become Who You Really Are* by Arthur F. Miller and William Hendricks, Copyright © 2002 by Arthur F. Miller and William Hendricks. Used by permission of Zondervan. www.zondervan.com.

12. John Bunyan, *The Pilgrim's Progress* (New York: P. F. Collier & Son, 1909), 78.

13. Jonathan Edwards, "The Preciousness of Time and the Importance of Redeeming It," in *The Works of Jonathan Edwards*, vol. 2 (London: F. Westley and A. H. Davis, 1835), xviii.

14. Lesslie Newbigin, *The Gospel in a Pluralist Society* (Grand Rapids: Eerdmans, 1989), 116. Used by permission.

15. Adapted from David J. Hesselgrave, *Planting Churches Cross-Culturally: North America and Beyond* (Grand Rapids: Baker Books, 2000). Used by permission.

16. Lesslie Newbigin, *The Household of God: Lectures on the Nature of the Church* (Eugene: Wipf and Stock, 2008), 25. Used by permission of Wipf and Stock Publishers, www.wipfandstock.com.

[17] The Lausanne Covenant, *"The Church and Evangelism,"* accessed from https://lausanne.org/content/covenant/lausanne-covenant#cov. Accessed on June 2, 2021.

[18] John Donne, *Devotions upon Emergent Occasions*, in The Works of John Donne, ed. Henry Alford (London: John W. Parker, 1839), 3: 575.

[19] Dietrich Bonhoeffer, *Life Together* (New York: Harper & Row Publishers, 1954), 26–27. From Life Together by Dietrich Bonhoeffer. English translation copyright © 1954 by Harper & Brothers, copyright renewed 1982 by Helen S. Doberstein. Used by permission of HarperCollins Publishers.

[20] C. H. Spurgeon, "A Faithful Friend," in *The New Park Street Pulpit Sermons*, vol. 3 (London: Passmore & Alabaster, 1857), 105–107.

[21] Adapted from the Mentoring Functions from *Connecting* by Paul D. Stanley and J. Robert Clinton. Copyright © 1992. Used by permission of NavPress, represented by Tyndale House Publishers. All rights reserved. Robert Clinton has pioneered research the fields of leadership development and mentoring relationships. Similar and related information can be found in Robert Clinton and Richard Clinton, *The Mentor Handbook: Detailed Guidelines and Helps for Christian Mentors and Mentorees* (Altadena: Barnabas Publishers, 1991).

[22] Martin Luther, *Large Catechism*, trans. John Nicholas Lenker (Minneapolis: The Luther Press, 1908), 44.

[23] Jonathan Edwards, "The Preciousness of Time and the Importance of Redeeming It," in *The Works of Jonathan Edwards*, vol. 2 (London: F. Westley and A. H. Davis, 1835), xviii.

[24] Adapted from Blaise Pascal, *Thoughts, Letters, and Minor Works*, ed. Charles W. Eliot, trans. W. F. Trotter, M. L. Booth, and O. W. Wight, The Harvard Classics 48 (New York: P. F. Collier & Son, 1910), 63–65.

[25] Adapted from Mortimer Adler, *Six Great Ideas* (New York: Touchstone, 1981). Adler suggested that *truth, goodness, and beauty* were three great ideas "we judge by" and *liberty, equality,* and *justice* were three great ideas "we live by." This six ideas suggested by Adler form a fitting framework for believers to evaluate *life values in light of God's priorities*.

[26] Thomas à Kempis, *Of the Imitation of Christ* (Oxford: Rivingtons, 1876), 2.

[27] J. Hudson Taylor, *China's Millions* (London: Morgan and Scott, 1890), 131.

[28] Elisabeth Elliot, *Discipline: The Glad Surrender* (Grand Rapids: Baker, 1982), 15–25. Used by permission.

[29] Adapted from Dallas Willard, *The Spirit of the Disciplines: Understanding How God Changes Lives* (New York, HarperCollins, 1988). Graphic adaptation of List of Disciplines, p. 158 of The Spirit of the Disciplines by Dallas Willard. Copyright © 1989 by Dallas Willard. Used by permission of HarperCollins Publishers.

[30] Isidore of Seville, *Sententiae* 3.8. The Latin text reads: *Qui vult cum deo semper esse, frequenter debet orare, frequenter et legere. nam cum oramus, cum deo ipsi loquimur; cum vero legimus, deus nobiscum loquitur.* Isidore of Seville, *Sententiae*, in Patrologiae cursus completus Series Latina, ed. J. P. Migne (Paris: Migne, 1862), 83:679.

[31] Thomas Watson, *A Body of Practical Divinity* (London: Thomas Parkhurst, 1692), 211.

[32] Gilbert K. Chesterton, *Orthodoxy* (New York: John Lane Company, 1909), 124.

[33] George Herbert, *Herbert's Poems* (New York: E. & J. B. Young and Company, 1903), 297.

About the Author

Matthew R. Lynskey, Ph.D. (2018), University of South Africa, serves in Training and Theological Formation at unfoldingWord. He is the author of Tyconius' Book of Rules (Brill, 2021) and of the modern church-based catechism series The Narrative Journey (Noble Imprint, forthcoming).

He has served in a variety of ministry capacities such as cross-cultural missionary, preaching pastor, church planter, and theological educator. Currently, he is an elder and Resident Theologian at Noble City Church and lives with his wife, Sukey, and their seven children in York, Pennsylvania.

www.ingramcontent.com/pod-product-compliance
Lightning Source LLC
Chambersburg PA
CBHW071147060526
44107CB00133B/340